Ten Minutes
to
Rake the Carpet

An Unexpected Life of
Hosting, Travel, Painting, and Politics

SHIRLEY HANSEN ACKER

Front cover photo by Fischer Photography

TEN MINUTES TO RAKE THE CARPET
AN UNEXPECTED LIFE OF HOSTING, TRAVEL, PAINTING, AND POLITICS

iUniverse books may be ordered through booksellers or by contacting:

iUniverse
1663 Liberty Drive
Bloomington, IN 47403
www.iuniverse.com
1-800-Authors (1-800-288-4677)

Because of the dynamic nature of the Internet, any web addresses or links contained in this book may have changed since publication and may no longer be valid. The views expressed in this work are solely those of the author and do not necessarily reflect the views of the publisher, and the publisher hereby disclaims any responsibility for them.

Any people depicted in stock imagery provided by Getty Images are models, and such images are being used for illustrative purposes only.
Certain stock imagery © Getty Images.

ISBN: 978-1-5320-7694-7 (sc)
ISBN: 978-1-5320-7693-0 (hc)
ISBN: 978-1-5320-7692-3 (e)

Library of Congress Control Number: 2019907038

Print information available on the last page.

iUniverse rev. date: 07/03/2019

Contents

Why This Book

Some who have written their memoirs have told me that doing so let them put their life in perspective. In writing, they could look back more objectively at the ups and downs, the excitement and the routine, the wins and the losses. Others say they wrote to fulfill an obligation, to give their children and grandchildren understanding of their life experience.

There is some of each in my case, but there is more. I want to share some uncommon experiences that I have been privileged to have, most of which I could not have dreamed of in my youth. By sharing, I hope to encourage readers, regardless of age, to reach out, to be willing to enter new territory, to accept and handle what comes, and to be confident and comfortable in new roles life may bring.

I also write to remind busy women pressured by their professions or other responsibilities that family and personal refreshment are high-level priorities. I therefore include some family activities, my painting, and some details of travel experience. Such pursuits help keep one's life on course and broaden one's perspective.

Especially, I write to express appreciation to the many who supported and encouraged me. Space allows listing only a few. Joan Shull, Marion Larson, Wy Johnson, Ruth Hostetler, and Janice Lee are among the many whose friendship gave me solid anchors during my years in the K-State president's home. I am also grateful to LaRayne Wahlstrom, Mary Helen Hopponen, and others with whom I worked closely in Brookings, South Dakota. Thanks also to neighbor and friend Jackie Woods and Betty Kiser in Ames, Nollie Bentley and Betsy Raposa in the White House Volunteer Office, Helen Blunk and others who taught and gave me confidence in my painting, and former governor Terry Branstad, at this writing US ambassador to China, who gave me challenging assignments after my husband's and my return to our

Iowa farm. Others, certainly including my parents and my good teachers, are mentioned or alluded to in the text.

For making copies of needed items I thank the staff at Choice Printing, Atlantic, and for the cover photo I am indebted to Sue Fischer, Fischer Photography, also of Atlantic.

For their encouragement and support in helping me complete this work, I especially appreciate my two daughters, Diane Acker Nygaard and LuAnn Acker, and my husband, Duane.

CHAPTER 1

Welcome to the President's Home

The doorbell rang a minute before two o'clock on a Saturday afternoon, and I opened the door to welcome the first of about two hundred guests, faculty and their spouses, to the Kansas State University president's home. Most I would be meeting for the first time; others were good friends from our time with the university a decade earlier.

There would be another group of two hundred that evening; two groups on Sunday, afternoon and evening; and yet another group a week later. I had been looking forward to these open houses since the previous April, when my husband, Duane, had been named by the Kansas Board of Regents to become K-State's eleventh president.

How important it had been to us during his years as a young faculty member at Oklahoma State and Iowa State to be invited to the department head's or dean's home, for us to be acknowledged, to be thought of as part of the department or college family. We had seen the same appreciation in the faces of students—Duane's advisees or fraternity and departmental club officers—invited in those years to our home. In time, as he had moved into administration, we had invited his college faculty and their spouses, as well as university friends, to our home on Manhattan's Oregon Lane in the early 1960s, our campus home during eight years at South Dakota State, and our later home in Lincoln, Nebraska.

I enjoyed the interaction with faculty, students, and university friends. It kept me in tune with all that was going on—the breadth of university disciplines, faculty and student concerns, and the university's dependence on political

1

and industry support. Our university life had been one of acquaintances and friendships, within and beyond the university. As a presidential couple, we would both enjoy and foster such relationships at K-State.

The house was ready, with living room, sunroom, and porch furniture in place and the dining room table loaded with cookies and bars that I had baked during the week. To make it more comfortable for all, the invitations had included staggered times, the first for 2:00 to 3:00 p.m. and the last for 4:00 to 5:00 p.m.

It was an especially rewarding afternoon for us, not only for the brief conversations but also for the pleasure that many long-term faculty and spouses expressed for having been invited. I yet recall greeting a senior professor of economics and his wife, two people who had been most gracious to us during our first tour at K-State. He was among several highly regarded and longtime faculty members who said, on our greeting, "Thanks for inviting us; we've never been in the president's home."

Midwesterners love to visit, lingering to share an experience or finish a story. After we bid goodbye to the last of the afternoon group, sometime after five, we picked up any napkins around the living room and sunroom before sitting down for a light dinner. By six forty-five the table was set with more cookies and bars, and I took a few minutes to rake the carpet before we were at the door to welcome the first of the evening groups.

* * * * *

Though Duane had been on the job since the first of July, his formal inauguration to the presidency was not until mid-September, early in the academic year. Held in Ahearn Field House, it was a festive occasion, with faculty in full academic regalia leading a procession that included representatives of other Kansas and conference or peer universities. There were welcoming comments by Governor Bob Bennett, Regent Chair Prudence Hutton (a K-State grad), and student body president Bernard Franklin. Many alumni, donors, legislators, and state organization people had come for the ceremony, and we enjoyed brief visits with all at a reception in the K-State Student Union following the ceremony.

We were especially complimented that friends from South Dakota State University (SDSU), the University of Nebraska, Iowa State, and Oklahoma State, as well as family and friends from our home area, had come for the event. And a good many stayed for the dance that evening. Because we enjoy dancing, the dance had been added to the agenda, unusual for a presidential inauguration, and alumni staff member Larry Weigel and his friends provided very danceable music.

The President's Home

Duane's predecessor, James A. McCain, had been in the presidency and he and his wife in the home for twenty-five years, and priorities for maintenance funds those years had been elsewhere, for classrooms and laboratories. Little had been invested in the 5,500-square-foot, three-story (plus basement) native-limestone house. The Kansas legislature had therefore appropriated money for renovation in early 1975, weeks before Duane was named.

The native-limestone house, constructed in the 1920s, was financed by a $25,000 gift from a Mr. and Mrs. Wilson. We found no public recognition of the Wilsons, so we chose to provide recognition by creating an address for the house, 100 Wilson Court. (Reprinted with permission of the Kansas State University Foundation.)

The wiring and the heating and air-conditioning system had to be replaced, and there would be a total redo of the kitchen and the second-floor baths, all to begin after the McCains' departure in late June. Consequently, on our arrival the last day of June, our furniture had been unloaded for storage in the home's double garage, and we were housed in a small apartment northeast of the campus that the university had leased.

Though I had helped Mrs. McCain serve for a women's group during our earlier years at K-State, Duane had never been in the house. University physical plant staff were doing the renovation and hoped to have the house ready for occupancy by the first of September. Unfortunately, that target was not met, and with the lease expired and the apartment committed to others, we found another temporary home. Two of our good friends, Director of International Programs Vern Larson and his wife, Marian, had invited us to occupy her vacationing mother's apartment.

As I had learned fourteen years earlier as our house on Manhattan's Oregon Lane, was being finished, I needed to be at the president's home most days to answer questions or to make decisions on paint color or other detail. Because my dad had been a painter and carpenter, I had empathy for the workers' tasks and enjoyed interacting with them. In fact, I could not resist stepping in to help (and perhaps quicken the job). I stripped some of the old wallpaper, painted the brick facing of the upstairs fireplace, and sanded the stair railing to the second floor.

The garage and the eating area of the kitchen were, in essence, a one-story extension at a forty-five-degree angle to the northeast. Early renovation steps had exposed a heavy iron beam that supported the northeast corner of the house's second and third stories, and the shipping notation, KSAC (Kansas State Agricultural College), on the beam was yet clear. Alan and Janice Lee, who, with Alan's brother, Robert, had built our house on Oregon Lane, suggested it would be architecturally interesting to leave that beam and the stone facing above it exposed. It would also allow an open ceiling for the area.

The kitchen had sufficient room for a small dining table, couch, TV, and telephone desk, and with addition of a small fireplace in the east corner, it would be a cozy and comfortable family area for Duane and me to spend the few evenings we might have at home.

Though work was still not done by inauguration day, it was far enough along that we could move from the apartment. Kitchen renovation was still underway, but some of the old cupboards had been moved to the basement, and we used the makeshift basement kitchen through November.

Designed for Entertaining

The house, built in the early 1920s, had been designed for entertaining. A large living room was off the entry foyer to the right. The living room opened also to a sunroom south of the foyer, and both the sun room and foyer opened to a dining room to the east, allowing for easy circulation of people. Off the sunroom to the east and south was a screened porch. Before returning to Kansas State, we had established a policy of no smoking in our house; smokers could use the porch. (We would receive many thank-yous from our guests for that policy.)

About the only bottleneck for handling large numbers, especially during the winter season, was the foyer's coat closet under the stairway; it was just too small. Our physical plant staff came to the rescue and fashioned a coatrack we could suspend from the ceiling in a nearby hallway. And because there were two steps up from the drive to the north side of our front porch, the physical plant staff would later install a sloping walk from the drive level up to the west side of our porch.

Though many universities provide a completely furnished president's home, with the furnishings often financed by a university foundation, such was not the case at K-State. Its foundation, then called the K-State Endowment Association, was yet a modest operation. Except for kitchen appliances, the house was empty.

We had accumulated considerable furniture but lacked several major pieces needed for both appearance and for entertaining. We purchased a large couch for one wall of the living room and a pair of red love seats that would look just right in front of the fireplace. My aunt Ada's refinished oak table and chairs (five dollars for the table and a dollar each for the chairs when purchased in the early 1900s) were perfect for the sunroom, and a wicker set—a love seat and two rockers that our daughter Diane had re-covered as a 4-H project—looked great on the screened-in porch. A tall oak secretary owned by Duane's grandfather would accommodate guest books in the foyer.

Greeting early guests in the house foyer, with the oak secretary of Duane's grandfather in the background. (Reprinted with permission of the Manhattan Mercury.)

In a previous paragraph I mentioned "raking" the carpet. Shag was in style at the time, 1975. In the late 1960s and early 1970s, in contrast to the tightly woven carpets of recent decades or of the 1950s, interior designers were exploring and recommending variations. By 1975, the rage was shag, with one- to two-inch lengths of eighth-inch-diameter fibers attached to a base. In some respects it was like a bluegrass lawn ready to be mowed! For the traffic we anticipated, I preferred and sought a more traditional, dense weave. However, what I sought was not available, at least not in the square yardage that was needed for the large living room, and we had to settle on a shag. It was a rich gold that complemented the red in our love seats and couches, and it was quite attractive until it got trampled by a hundred, or even a few, walking on it.

I soon learned that to put the shag fibers back in place, somewhat upright and with uniform appearance, even if only I had walked through the living room to fetch a book, I would need to rake the carpet. Yes, the carpet shops provided a long-handled rake, and after some practice, I could get all the fibers at least leaning the same direction.

The home had a maid's quarters, with a bedroom and bath, on the second floor, and a back stairway led from it to the kitchen and basement. However, there was no maid in the university budget. That fact did not bother me; I had plenty of energy and had always done my own housework as well as considerable entertaining without hired help. With the maid's quarters available and with our success in having a student live with us in our SDSU campus home, we decided to invite a student to live in those quarters in exchange for some modest help, mostly cleaning and helping me prepare for hosting. She would be close to her classes and could take her meals on campus. Further, it would be good to have a person in the house during our absence for night events and travel.

Fall Commitments

During the fall months it seemed that virtually every evening had been committed, full of dinners with students, alumni, or industry or community groups. An example was the week of October 5. For that week, the only day without commitment, according to our calendar from that time, was Sunday. Monday night we had dinner with alumni in Hutchinson, Tuesday night with alumni in Hays, Wednesday with the Pi Phi fraternity near campus, and Thursday evening with the Restaurant Management Student Club. Friday at five o'clock we were at Dean Don Rathbone's home with his College of Engineering advisory committee, and at six we had dinner at the Union with the Agricultural Education Club. Saturday we hosted several legislators and visiting Iowa State folks in the "president's box" for a 1:30 Big Eight football game, and that evening was a girls' volleyball game followed by an 8:30 dessert at the home of one of our faculty leaders.

The Football Season, then Basketball

For football, our "president's box" was a block of twenty seats in the back two rows of the central section of West Stadium. For each home game we would invite to these seats key alumni, legislators, donors, the visiting team's university president, and, when hosting the University of Kansas, our Kansas governor and wife. Though we were protected from chilly October and November winds only by a block wall behind us, our location let us greet fans as well as watch the play.

The higher-level press box was, in 1975, rather modest, just enough space for writers and a few assistant coaches or spotters who communicated with coaches on the sidelines. It was far less spacious and comfortable than what we had enjoyed at Nebraska or what was to come later at Kansas State.

Kansas was yet a dry state. Though all knew beer, wine, and mixed drinks were not uncommon in parking lot tailgating, the halftime refreshment served in the president's box by student ambassadors was limited to 7 Up and Coke.

December brought the basketball season. With the popularity of K-State basketball among students, townspeople, and alumni, we never missed a home game, unless Duane was out of town. The two of us would walk up past Anderson Hall about six thirty on game nights to our spot in the west bleachers of Ahearn Field House.

Women's basketball was then only emerging in popularity and was fighting for fans, use of facilities, and recognition by the donor community. Much progress would be made during our tenure, including even a doubleheader, a women's game preceding the men's. More detail on the decade-long effort to ensure equal opportunity for women's sports is provided in Duane's memoir *Two at a Time*.

Beginning the day after Christmas, we would be in Kansas City for the Big Eight men's basketball tournament. The games would be in Kansas City's Kemper Arena, and we would host or be hosted by a few key alumni at dinner in the Alameda Plaza. A few days later we would fly to Miami for the Orange Bowl.

The Orange Bowl

By contract, the Big Eight Conference football champion played in Miami's Orange Bowl each year, and the conference's annual meeting, involving both athletic directors and presidents, was held at the time of the bowl. It was therefore both an obligation and an opportunity for us to spend a few days at the beachside Sea View Hotel in Bal Harbour on Miami Beach, to be hosted by members of the bowl sponsoring committee to receptions and boat rides, and, of course, to enjoy the Oklahoma-Michigan game the night of January 1. With our daughters, Diane and LuAnn, home from their universities for Christmas break, we all flew to Miami and enjoyed a couple of afternoons on the beach.

We flew back to Kansas Friday evening, January 2, ready for a busy schedule. We attended a reception for Manhattan's chamber of commerce director Sunday night, went to dinner with Japanese visitors in the Union

Tuesday night, and hosted a series of faculty groups and others in our home in the days that followed.

Except for a couple of three-day weekends at our Iowa farm home and the week of Christmas Day, any random selection of a week during our first twelve months in the president's home might yield a comparable schedule. And these events were in addition to my daytime household and social activities plus, when I could, noon-hour lap swimming at the university natatorium. It was good that we were yet in our forties with energy and good health. It would only be the following June, after spring commencement, when we might count on two or three evenings a week at home without a university-related social commitment.

Our First Guests

It was early December before the house renovation was complete and the kitchen ready to use. Because I had enjoyed and appreciated the physical plant workers and their quality work, they and their wives would be our first guests. I wanted all, including those who had done only some of the early work, to see the finished product and to be able to show it to their wives. For them to see and to enjoy some refreshments in the renovated president's home was another way to express our praise and thanks for their outstanding work.

Next in priority were the people with whom Duane worked and would work on a daily basis—vice presidents, deans, and directors, along with their spouses, and their secretaries as well. (All know that a unit's head secretary is key to that unit's smooth functioning.) For their convenience, we invited the secretaries for a 4:30 tea on Friday, December 12, and the following Sunday evening, December 14, it was the vice presidents, deans, and directors.

As a land-grant university, K-State had faculty and staff located across the state, in county and area extension offices and at branch agricultural experiment stations. Only at the time of a statewide conference on campus could we host any portion as a group. The annual experiment station conference was scheduled for the first week of January, so we hosted all experiment station staff the evening of Wednesday, January 7, at 8:30 p.m., following their staff dinner.

That was also the case for leaders of the K-State Alumni Association, an organization very effective in supporting the university, both financially and politically, as well as in encouraging young men and women to enroll.

Association directors would be on campus for a couple of days in February, so we scheduled dessert and coffee at the president's home on Friday, February 20, at 8:00 p.m., for directors, staff, and spouses.

For Friday evening, January 16, we had arranged what might be called an event of personal privilege, hosting eight couples, Manhattan friends with whom we had become especially close during our earlier four years at K-State.

I had many other friends of old in Manhattan, including Oregon Lane neighbors Joan Shull and Janice Lee, Rae Stamey and Evelyn Schoeff of my former bridge club, and several parents of our daughters' Marlatt grade school classmates. There were also members of Trinity Presbyterian Church, which we had attended, and of the faculty women's club. Their friendship and presence had helped make it an easy move and adjustment to our new role.

Commencement

Each year, spring commencement was a full two-day event, including a Friday-afternoon reception in our home for alumni honorees and their families, those receiving honorary doctorates, and visiting commencement speakers. Perhaps my favorite was hosting fifty-year graduates. For fall or summer commencements, which involved smaller numbers and were more limited in time, we usually hosted some form of reception.

As I Write These Words Forty Years Later

During our eleven years in the K-State president's home, we hosted more receptions and open houses than I gave thought to at the time. It was simply a part of our life and role. Beyond those for faculty and others already mentioned were those for the student government association, clubs, fraternity and sorority housemothers, and a few state or national groups that held conventions or scientific meetings on the K-State campus. We wanted to host these groups. It was not only the purpose of a state university president's home; it was one of the functions of a presidential couple.

We were also hosted more and treated more generously, more often, and by more wonderful people than one could list, including alumni, fraternities, sororities, other residence groups, Manhattan townspeople, industry groups, and Kansas communities statewide.

I had the privilege of being involved in more worthy community efforts than would have been possible in other life settings.

We traveled more and saw more of this great country and of the world (as well as of Kansas) than I had dreamed of during my youth.

In a later chapter, I share more details of our life in and from the K-State president's home, describing some of our interesting and rewarding experiences in the decade that followed this first year. Chapters 2 and 3 describe the path from our March 1952 marriage, to our life in five campus communities and raising two wonderful daughters, to June 30, 1975, when we unloaded our furniture at the Kansas State University president's home.

CHAPTER 2

Embracing the University Life

It was Wednesday morning, March 26, 1952. Our first home, the west half of a Quonset in the post-WWII veterans' village, Pammel Court, on the north edge of the Iowa State University campus, was newly painted, clean, and ready. After Duane's graduation the previous Friday; our Sunday wedding in the Methodist church of our hometown, Atlantic, Iowa; and a two-day honeymoon in Des Moines, we had arrived to what would be our home for the next eighteen months.

During nights in the last weeks of winter quarter, Duane had painted the Quonset walls, walls that blended into and became ceilings. Pammel management had provided only two colors of paint, crème and light green, so Duane had splurged and purchased a gallon of white for the kitchen area. I would only need to fix some curtains for the small windows; those for the windows on the sloping side walls would be held in place by light springs threaded through their upper and lower seams.

*Our honeymoon cottage, 234 Pammel Court. The former WWII
Quonset provided two apartments; ours faced the university's Veenker golf
course. Iowa State's biotechnology building now occupies the site.*

Our front door opened to the first fairway of the golf course, and we enjoyed the view. However, we were on the slice side of that fairway, so we were sometimes awakened or at least surprised on weekend mornings by a ball hitting the Quonset and rat-a-tatting down the corrugated siding. Since the unit was not air-conditioned, we often left the side windows open during the day, and if a strong wind came up during the day, we sometimes returned to find a light layer of cinder dust from the Pammel drives on our furniture.

Our five-hundred-square-foot home, four rooms and bath, was heated by an oil stove. Our phone was in a booth a half block away. It was a modest home, but good neighbors made Pammel a fun place to live.

During his undergraduate years, Duane had developed an intense interest in animal nutrition and would be working toward a master's degree, with his target to be a nutritionist in the animal feed industry. His to-be major professor, Damon Catron, had offered me a typing job in his office.

My job in Catron's office, which was in the north wing of the main floor of Curtiss Hall, was largely typing abstracts that graduate students had hand copied from research papers in nutrition and biochemistry journals, dittoing copies of the abstracts for staff and graduate students, and placing staff members' copies in their notebooks. The purpose was to help all keep in touch with new research findings in animal nutrition and to have handy references for any nutrition-related issue. Having worked three years with an animal feed company, calculating salesmen's commissions on product sold, I felt comfortable and reasonably familiar with the terminology.

We Start a Family

Our daughter Diane was born the following February 15 by cesarean at Mary Greeley Hospital in Ames. The annual spring FarmHouse formal dance was but a few days after Diane and I came home from the hospital. Duane and I love to dance, and I was determined to go. Former farm neighbor Cliff Christensen, who was attending the college's winter short course, came out to our Quonset home to babysit Diane. She apparently slept through the evening while Duane and I enjoyed the dance.

I had resigned my job to care for Diane but took on several typing jobs, working at home. The first was typing soil analysis reports prepared for clients of the university soil-testing lab. Next, Professor Clarence Bundy, then revising his high school animal husbandry text, asked me to type several manuscript sections for him.

All were great experiences, especially for one whose future life, unexpected at the time, would be in university settings. I had become acquainted with all animal science faculty, most of the department's graduate students, and a few undergraduates and had developed a comfortable feel for the total university.

To Oklahoma

Duane completed his master's degree the following August and lined up an instructor position at Oklahoma State University (then Oklahoma A&M) in Stillwater. We drove to Stillwater in early August for an interview, and he was offered and accepted the job, which would allow him to also work on his PhD in nutrition, his target yet the animal feed industry. We rented a two-bedroom bungalow two blocks north of the campus, at 524 Bellis Drive (that area has now been covered by expanded OSU athletic facilities).

For our early-September move to Stillwater, we packed our modest furniture in Duane's dad's pickup and a towed U-Haul. My parents followed by car and stayed a couple of days to help us get settled. Important in what we took from Ames were bags of green and half-ripe tomatoes from our Iowa

State swine-nutrition farm garden, with the bags stuffed in any available space in the 1949 Ford's trunk. We were both happy and frugal.

We were impressed by Oklahoma friendliness; the animal husbandry staff and spouses were most generous and welcoming. Our landlord, a Mr. Gossett, lived but a block away and invited us and another of his nearby tenants, the Gilstrap family, to his home every Wednesday night to watch Arthur Godfrey on television. We had no TV set, and that was our week's social highlight.

FarmHouse fraternity alumni were also welcoming. Duane had been a member of the Iowa State chapter. The group met monthly at the fraternity house on North Washington, and most played bridge. We had not yet learned the game, and when we mentioned that, two of the group, OSU president Oliver Willham and his wife, suggested we play hearts instead. The Willhams' thoughtful consideration meant so much, and we would appreciate their continued friendship and support.

The Willhams' son, Richard, was then a senior in animal husbandry and a member of the intercollegiate meats judging team, for which Duane served as assistant coach. On graduation, Richard moved to Iowa State for graduate study in animal genetics and, years later, would return to Iowa State's faculty.

Duane was busy teaching freshman animal husbandry courses as well as helping with a junior-level meat-processing course during the academic year. He was also enrolled in one graduate course each semester and, being on only a ten-month appointment, took two or three courses during the summer.

Within a few months we began looking for a small house to buy; we would rather build equity than pay rent. By January we found a small two-bedroom home west of the campus, and borrowed money from my dad for the down payment. It had a fenced-in backyard, an attached garage, and a small but adequate laundry room for my automatic washer.

Not long after moving to 2129 Sherwood Drive (now Sherwood Avenue), we were looking forward to the birth of our second daughter, LuAnn. This birth, too, would be by cesarean, so we could set the time. LuAnn was due to arrive the morning of September 14.

Knowing the birth date allowed my sister Norma Jean to drive my mother down ahead of time to be there to take care of Diane and to make sure Duane had enough to eat. September 14 was a day of record-breaking heat—114 degrees. When Duane came to visit LuAnn and me in the air-conditioned hospital room late in the afternoon, after mixing feed for his research lambs, he nearly fell asleep in the cool comfort.

My mother's maternal relatives—the Kites—in Blackwell, Oklahoma, learned she was in town, and they drove down for the day after I returned from the hospital. We were pleased they would come, and I, determined that the house be clean for visitors, spent my first morning home cleaning the living and dining room floors.

There were many young families in the neighborhood, and I was invited to join a child study group for young mothers. I easily made many friends in the group, two being the wife of the college beef herdsman, Al Rutledge, and the wife of Duane's biochemistry instructor and dean of the graduate school, Dr. Bob MacVicar.

Back to Iowa State and Ames

Near the end of our second summer at Oklahoma A&M, in 1955, Duane was invited back to teach in Iowa State's animal husbandry department. Having completed what are called "residence requirements," a certain number of credits on the A&M campus, he could earn additional needed graduate credits at Iowa State, transfer them back, and, in time, receive his PhD from OSU. By then, it was clear we both enjoyed life in a university community. We had chaperoned both fraternity and sorority parties and had students to our home, and Duane had found teaching and advising students highly rewarding.

We drove to Ames for his interview. His first year's salary at Iowa State would not be much above that at OSU, but with several faculty near retirement, the opportunity was too good to pass up. Beyond that, the move would take us back to our home state, closer to our parents and, for our daughters, closer to their grandparents.

Our parents were delighted with our plans, and while we focused on selling our house in Stillwater, the four of them drove the 110 miles to Ames more than once to locate a rental home for us. In time, they found a near-new, two-bedroom country home just two miles from Ames and a half mile west of Ontario. It had a large enough basement that we could rent space to four graduate students, and with the house came a large black Lab, an outdoor playmate for our daughters. With our daughters not yet in school, we could get along with one car, which Duane would drive to campus.

My automatic washer also ended up in the basement. One morning I was busy with the washing, and all was quiet upstairs, unusually quiet. In time, I found out why: my two angels were also creative, and they were drawing with crayons on the hallway wall. We got the wall cleaned, and they did not do that again!

We joined the Presbyterian Church, located just outside the campus's west gate, and became active in a young couples' group, the Dinghy Club, which met monthly at the church for evening programs. As a club, we painted the nursery school on a Saturday, sold Christmas trees each December on a drive behind the church, and often had social events in members' homes. I helped in the church nursery and with our daughters' Sunday school, and Duane served as a deacon, ushering and taking sermon tape recordings to shut-ins.

Though the farm home was comfortable, we searched for a home within walking distance to the campus and to a school; Diane would be ready for kindergarten in 1958.

We looked at many houses with realtors and eventually learned through a faculty colleague that Dr. J. B. Davidson, the retired head of agricultural engineering, and his wife would be selling their home, which was about four blocks south of the campus and within two blocks of Louise Crawford Elementary School. We immediately called and arranged a visit. The story-and-a-half Cape Cod would fit our needs perfectly, and it was even air-conditioned, a rarity at the time. We went as a family to see the home, and Mrs. Davidson fell in love with our two little girls. Perhaps they reminded her of her two daughters at those ages.

The house had a full basement, including shower and toilet facilities, so those four graduate students could move with us when we took possession in August. The north half of the basement would accommodate my laundry and a small workshop for Duane.

Dr. and Mrs. Gilkey owned a vacant lot adjacent to the Davidson house to the east, and on that lot they had a small garden. In early summer they invited us to use a portion of the garden space, so we would have some garden produce when we moved in.

By the end of our first year at 2329 Storm Street, the rental income from those four graduate students had let us pay off the loan from my aunt we had needed for the house down payment. The students had completed their degrees, so we disposed of the bunk beds, desks, and chests; tiled the floor in the walled-off half they had used; and repainted the walls. This space would be our family room.

I like to paint and could not resist extending the basement redecorating. The rather plain wall of the storage space below the stairs bothered me, and the laundry/bath area also needed brightening up. After another half day I had a bright wall, painted with vertical red and white six-inch stripes. I would enjoy those bright stripes for the balance of the six years we would live in the house.

Schools, Books, and Ballet

With Louise Crawford Elementary School just around the corner and three blocks up Hayward Street, I could walk with Diane—and the next year also LuAnn—to the Hayward corner and watch her walk to kindergarten.

Our daughters' school was important. I agreed to be secretary of the Parent-Teacher Association (PTA), was homeroom mother for each of our girls, and accompanied their teachers and classes on a field trip to the Des Moines airport.

Both Diane and LuAnn took ballet lessons. They were so cute in their little ballet tutus at their annual dance recital. Diane was not so fond of ballet, but LuAnn would continue with it after our later move to Manhattan, Kansas. She loved dancing and was very graceful.

Both girls loved to read, and at least once a week, we would drive home from the public library with our car's back seat loaded with books.

Our Storm Street house was a wonderful family home, in part because of the friendly families in adjacent homes—the Gibbons, he an economics instructor; the Lorches, he head of the department of English; and, in time, Walt and Jackie Woods, OSU friends. Walt had joined the animal husbandry department two years after our arrival. Across the street were, first, an animal husbandry couple, Vaughn and Meg Speer, and, later, Virgil and Jackie Hays (Virgil had been a senior at OSU our first semester there). Across the intersection were Associate Dean Roy and Wanda Kottman.

Our family preparing for a camping trip in July, 1961. The fold-out camping trailer was built by my brother-in-law Glenn Owen Jones.

I joined the Faculty Wives' Social Club, of course, and recall having the club decorations committee use our basement Ping-Pong table to lay out the materials for the decorations and for a table centerpiece. Among those workers was the wife of Iowa State vice president and future president Bob Parks. All, especially Mrs. Parks, were so friendly and helpful.

My husband and I had avoided learning bridge; we had seen and heard of novices unduly chastised and unnerved when they played the wrong card. However, after the Woods' arrival to a rental house next door, they taught us the elements, and we were invited to join a couples' club comprised of animal husbandry department colleagues. We thoroughly enjoyed the group—and the game. In fact, we formed a second bridge club, in this case inviting couples from varied occupations. Among them were Harold and Alma Schiel, he with the Iowa Department of Transportation, and Chuck and Joan Frederiksen, natives respectively of Exira and Adair, Iowa. Chuck was then assistant director of housing for the university.

We had also joined a town-and-gown formal dance group, Red Friars, which, at least during the winter season, danced monthly in the university's Memorial Union.

A Club for Students' Wives

Quite a few animal husbandry students (then essentially all young men) were married, and several of their wives had expressed need for interaction with others, so Bettie Kiser, whose husband was also on the faculty, and I helped them get organized as the "Animal Science Student Wives." Through this group, these young women could become acquainted and compare notes on jobs and families. In essence, it was a mutual support group, and the relationships they established would be helpful to both the wives and the students. Betty and I would often host the group in our homes, and it would usually turn out to be a late night; they so enjoyed the interaction and hated to leave.

By the start of Duane's and my fourth year at Iowa State, it had become clear we had chosen the university life. Dean Floyd Andre had asked Duane to head the farm-operation curriculum, about six hundred majors planning to return to the farm. He continued to teach an animal science course (the department had changed its name from "husbandry" to "science") each quarter.

It seemed to me a student wives' group was needed here also, so I invited several of the farm-operation student wives to our house and helped them organize. It also seemed appropriate for us to host a reception for farm-operation graduates, in our backyard for spring and summer graduation or in our house for fall and winter. The wives' group, by then full of members enjoying each other, was eager to help make arrangements and host. It was a great experience for me to work with these young women.

In the fall of 1961, Andre and animal science department head Leslie Johnson invited Duane to join them for most of November to review and recommend some agricultural education programs in Argentina. Though he did not speak Spanish, this proved to be a valuable experience, especially for the leadership learning experience of working with Andre and Johnson.

Saturday morning after Duane's return, he found at his office a letter from Dean Glenn Beck at Kansas State University, in Manhattan, Kansas, saying Duane had been recommended for an associate dean position there. It would involve leadership of the College of Agriculture's teaching, curriculum development, and academic advising of students.

To Kansas?

Yes, Duane was interested! We drove to Manhattan in mid-December for a two-day visit with Beck, the college department heads, and other key people, and all appeared mutually positive. However, Duane could not be formally offered the position because the university president, James A. McCain, was ill and unavailable—and Beck was soon departing for a month-long trip to review programs in Africa. It would be March before schedules allowed Duane to go to Manhattan by train for a second visit and a formal offer and acceptance. We would be moving to Manhattan, Kansas, on June 1, 1962.

Selling our Ames house was a joyous experience. The wife of the couple who had built the house saw our For Sale ad in the *Ames Tribune* and called. She told me their story of having built the house in 1939, the first of several they had planned to build for sale. They were proud of the house's quality, but it had turned out to also be the last house they would build. We had to assume it had not been sold at a profit.

Now was a chance for them to re-own the house and, having retired from another occupation, enjoy it! A few nights later, they sat with us in our living room to negotiate a price. Her tears flowed when we reached an agreement; they had bought "their home." They could return to the product of their labor. They were happy, and we were happy for them.

CHAPTER 3

On the Road Again

For us, it was again house-hunting time, and it required two trips to Manhattan. On the first, we looked at a number of homes and found a two-story colonial near both a grade school and the high school and at a price we could handle. The only problem was that the owner had promised another party, "If we ever sell, we will give you first chance." However, the other party had recently purchased a home, seemed well settled, and likely would decline. We returned to Ames with confidence. A few days later, though, came a disappointing letter: the other party was purchasing the house.

So it was back to Manhattan. Having scouted the town earlier and having looked and passed on other houses, we sought advice from former Ames friends, the John Nordins, who were in a newly constructed home about a mile northwest of the campus. They introduced us to their builders, the Lee brothers, and after reviewing plans and costs, we contracted for a house then being framed up at 2802 Oregon Lane, across the street from the Nordins. It would be finished by August. We then rented a small furnished house on Ellis Drive, just west of the campus, for the interim, effective June 1.

Our family at the mailbox of 2802 Oregon Lane,
Manhattan, just before Christmas, 1962.

John and June Nordin were wonderful neighbors and friends for years. The same pertains to Paul and Joan Shull and their children, Mike, Terry, and Kevin, who lived next door to the Nordins. Paul was the K-State band director and Joan a great organist. At this writing, Joan is still a special friend.

Room Mother Again

Diane and LuAnn, then ready for fourth and third grades, would walk south on Claflin about three blocks to Marlatt Elementary School. For LuAnn's fourth-grade class, our second year in Manhattan, I became room mother. It was a challenging time. In early fall school officials judged her class too large, and the principal, Mr. McArthur, expressed intent to relocate part of her class to College Hill Elementary, an older school several blocks to the north. Both the students and their mothers were upset, fearing they would lose their great teacher Mrs. Muncie. I offered our house for a meeting of mothers and invited Mr. McArthur. He came and listened, and the move was dropped.

A Hosting Role

There was no job description for the wife of an associate dean, but we had observed at both Oklahoma State and Iowa State the value of hosting students and faculty in one's home; it showed interest, support, and, especially for faculty, recognition of people and their work. Because Duane's big push was to strengthen the academic advising program, our first effort was to invite, in groups, all the college's academic advisers and their spouses. With each group we included deans of other colleges or staff from admissions, student affairs, or the counseling center—people those advisers should know.

The involvement of the college's department heads was important to that student advising effort, so we invited them as well as Dean Beck and spouses to a coffee prior to the fall student dance, called the Barnwarmer. The timing made it logical that they might go as a group to the Barnwarmer, showing their personal interest in the students at this major student function.

Obviously, I baked a lot of cookies and served these with punch and sometimes also coffee.

The college student council sponsored an annual dance, and that included a queen competition. So we invited the council members, each accompanying a queen candidate, to our home for a Sunday-afternoon reception—more cookies and punch.

Industry and Professional Connections

Our relationships were not limited to students and faculty. The college worked closely with dozens of industry groups related to the state's agriculture, many of them contributing student scholarship or research funds. Evening dinners at the K-State Union and events in Topeka, Salina, and Wichita were part of our life. An example relationship was that with Farmland Industries, a regional cooperative headquartered in Kansas City but with member cooperatives throughout Kansas and neighboring states.

Two of our summers in Manhattan, our family spent a week in June at Farmland Industries' Family Camp at the YMCA Camp just outside of Estes Park, Colorado. Duane had been invited to give a five-minute "eye-opener" presentation each morning to the cooperative managers and directors from Farmland's seven-state area (and any family that wanted to attend the morning program). For the balance of each day, we joined other attendees for area tours or barbecues, and the girls could swim or join in other youth activities.

Duane also needed to retain relationships in his discipline, animal science.

Consequently, in August 1964, we saw both the Rockies and a bit of the Appalachians. We got back to Manhattan from the Farmland Industries' Family Camp on a Saturday afternoon and left the next morning for the animal science summer meetings at the University of Tennessee. We saw more of our country's beauty, visited with our animal science family friends from several campuses, and enjoyed an evening barbecue in the Smokies. On our drive home we visited the well-known Berea College in Kentucky.

June 1965 gave another family travel opportunity. To promote a new bakery management curriculum at K-State, the baking industry had invited Duane to speak at the Canadian Bakers' Association meeting in Quebec City. We flew to Quebec, stayed at Hotel Frontenac, visited the adjacent Plains of Abraham, toured the city by bus, and then rented a car to drive down the Saint Lawrence River to the northeast and around the midriver Isle of Orleans. On the way home, we spent a weekend in Toronto. Our daughters were surprised that only churches and parks—no stores nor movies—were open on Sunday. We walked the underground shopping areas, visited a park, and flew home on Monday in time to greet attendees at a meat science conference on the K-State campus. (Duane had taught and done research on meat processing and quality at Oklahoma State, so he had many friends among the attendees.)

A New 4-H Club

There was no 4-H club in our Manhattan neighborhood, so I called the assistant Riley County extension agent, Jim Smith, and asked whether there was a club that our girls could join. There was no club in the area, but if we could identify some leaders, we could start one. Carl Menzies, member of the animal science faculty, and a dietician who lived nearby said they would work with the girls. Together, we organized the Valley High 4-H Club, with ten members.

To South Dakota?

In the fall of 1965, South Dakota State University in Brookings needed a new dean for the College of Agriculture and Biological Science. SDSU president Hilton Briggs, along with Oscar Olsen, interim dean and chair of

Briggs's search committee, drove to Manhattan to interview each of Beck's three associates for the position, one being Duane and the other two being leaders of research and extension. They arranged a lunch, dinner, or breakfast with each candidate and his spouse; ours was a dinner at Keck's Steak House east of Manhattan. Briggs was an Iowa State FarmHouse alum, and Duane had met him fifteen years earlier at a University of Wyoming FarmHouse chapter installation, where Briggs was then dean of agriculture. Later, while we were at Iowa State, Duane had had two of Briggs's nephews as students.

At dinner, Briggs ordered a New York strip and told us why he preferred that cut. I ordered a small fillet. When we were served, the waitress gave Briggs my fillet and me his New York strip. Briggs was so busy telling us about South Dakota State that he did not notice, and soon he was eating my steak! I did not say a word; it was too late.

The next morning Briggs stopped by a class Duane was teaching and said he wanted the two of us to come to Brookings as soon as it could be arranged to talk more about the deanship. Our whole family was enjoying Manhattan and loved our friends there, but the job would be a great opportunity. We drove to Brookings in mid-October for a formal interview and to meet department heads and other college leaders and spouses, and a few days later we knew we would be moving to Brookings.

With the dean position came a large house on the north side of the SDSU campus. Both Duane's position and the campus home suggested a broader role for me, especially the hosting of faculty, students, and friends and supporters of the college.

The day after Thanksgiving we picked up Duane's parents in Iowa and drove to Brookings to check out the house. Interim Dean Olsen and Dr. Al Musson, who was assistant director of the experiment station (and would prove to be Duane's most valuable and appreciated administrative colleague), met us at the house, told us they planned to redecorate, and asked for our ideas. There had been a heavy snow, and the house was empty and cold. However, we quickly saw it could be a friendly and comfortable home. It had large living and dining rooms; an expansive, glass-enclosed front porch; and four bedrooms and two baths on the second floor.

After a generous dinner and visit hosted by the Olsens in their home that evening, we checked in to our rooms at the Brookings Hotel. About two in the morning, all of us in deep sleep under heavy blankets, the phone rang. "Please come down and move your car so the snowplow can clear the street." It was a chilling introduction to the reality of a Brookings winter.

With four bedrooms in that campus home, perhaps we could have a college student live with us. Duane's work would involve many evening dinners for both of us, and there would also be out-of-town events requiring overnight stays. With our daughters at the middle school stage, it would be good to have an older girl in the home. Musson quickly found an SDSU coed, Virginia Luckhurst, who was well referenced and interested. She was ready to move in when we arrived, February 1, the beginning of spring semester. This turned out to be a wonderful arrangement. In exchange for a bit of help with the house, Virginia received a room within walking distance of classes and a dining hall where she could take her meals.

Unfortunately, in one of the first weeks of the semester, Virginia fell on the ice and broke a leg. I then drove her to and from her campus classes until her leg healed.

Our family in front of our Brookings home, the dean's house on the north edge of the South Dakota State University campus, 1966.

During our eight years at SDSU, we would have three young women in this arrangement. We still correspond with Junia Meyer, who was with us the longest and is now retired after a teaching career in a South Dakota high school.

Our Daughters' Schools

The middle of the school year, between semesters, proved to be a good moving time for Diane and LuAnn. The middle school principal in Brookings asked another seventh grader to show Diane to her assigned classrooms, orient her to her new surroundings, and introduce her to other classmates. The two became good friends. Both Diane and LuAnn adapted quickly to their new school.

The middle school was near downtown; a new high school, yet under construction when we arrived, was on the south edge of Brookings; and our campus home was on the north edge. Though a school bus carrying rural students passed our home morning and evening, our daughters were not eligible to ride because our home was inside the city limits. Consequently, I drove the girls to school every day and picked them up after, often giving some of their friends rides as well. This turned out to be valuable; I became acquainted with their friends and where they lived, and I learned at the end of each school day all that had happened.

Fortunately, the new high school had a large swimming pool, and when a lifesaving class was offered a few years after our arrival, I enrolled and later passed the lifesaving test. I was both pleased and proud to have earned a livesaving certificate.

February in South Dakota

As suggested to us during our November visit to the campus, we had an electric soft plug heater installed in our car engine. With the heater plugged in at night, the car would start more easily in the morning. However, the interior of the car was still frigid. Within weeks Duane installed a second electric heater, under the dash. The cords for both heaters extended through the car grill, and I could plug them into a timer each afternoon, with the timer set for 6:00 a.m. I could then drive the girls to school in a warm car.

Our drive was on the north, shady side of the house, so packed snow or ice was common. One day, new friend LaRayne Wahlstrom arrived at our north door, as she had invited me to ride with her to a church event. She told me later that she watched me rush out the door and around the front of her car—and then I disappeared! Just as I was about to grab her car door handle, my feet hit some ice and went out from under me, and I virtually slid under her car. Not a very gracious way to meet a new friend.

Our Church

The Methodist Church became our church home in Brookings, and as the girls reached high school, Duane and I were asked to take the leadership of the church youth group. I would call this a challenging joy and highly rewarding. A younger couple, Paula and Larry Jorgensen, joined us as coleaders, and youth from other churches, especially several of our daughters' friends, became regular participants. Each Sunday evening we met at the church for programs, outside speakers, fellowship, and fun.

The group was eager to raise money, and we embarked on several efforts, with parents jumping in to help. We fried and delivered doughnuts on a Saturday morning and churned homemade ice cream for a Sunday ice cream social. In the latter case, one boy was yet cranking his freezer long after others' contents had hardened. He had failed to put in the paddle!

A highlight for the group was a Sunday at Blue Cloud Abbey northeast of Watertown, South Dakota. We all had lunch with the brothers and learned of their life and work and some of their reasons for choosing the abbey life.

Duane and I had equipped our basement with a pool table, Ping-Pong table, couches, chairs, and a refrigerator for soft drinks. Those amenities and plenty of popcorn made it an attractive place for the church youth group as well as other of Diane's and LuAnn's friends. We would often invite some of the parents for an upstairs party and perhaps to play bridge.

Our daughters could handle their parents being leaders of their youth group, but when I was asked, in an early-Sunday phone call, to fill in as a counselor at a weeklong church camp to begin that afternoon, it was, for a time, too much! Their immediate reaction was "Oh, no!" However, by the time we were dressed for church, they had reconsidered and were urging me to call back my acceptance.

Serving as a camp counselor was a rewarding experience. Some campers were away from home for the first time. I spent time with an especially homesick young girl, and when her parents were delayed at the close of camp, she came home with us to await her parents.

As a part of the Methodist Church, we had a women's care group, which met each Tuesday morning and identified those members—or nonmembers—who needed help in their home or maybe just someone to stop in for a visit. Our minister often provided a list of names. I recall a couple who were about to celebrate their fiftieth anniversary but did not have the health or energy to arrange and host a party. Our group took on the task and helped plan and carry out the party, including serving anniversary cake to their guests. For us, there was a wonderful feeling of giving.

Most of our visits, though, were just that: visits. We were someone to be greeted, to exchange friendly and cheerful conversation, and to show interest. We would usually return to the church with stories of satisfaction and good feelings of having cared for someone else. We could also pass along to our minister information that would be helpful in planning his visits.

PEO

I was invited to join the Brookings chapter of PEO (Chapter BA) in early 1967, a year after we had arrived in Brookings, and soon had many friends among the membership. The PEO affiliation would become especially valuable as we moved on to other locations. While writing these memoirs, now a member of Chapter AF in Atlantic, Iowa, I was awarded my fifty-year recognition pin. Between Brookings and Atlantic, I have enjoyed membership in four other chapters: CS in Lincoln, Nebraska; BD in Manhattan, Kansas; and two, AO and G, in the Washington, DC, area.

Record Snow and a Full Day

The morning of January 29, 1969 (my birthday and the week of semester exams), the streets were slick, and snow was piled so high on each side of the street that one could not see other cars at intersections. (We had seventy inches of snow that winter, likely a record.) I was taking our daughters and one of their friends to the high school, and as we were moving south through an intersection, our car was hit from the right by an SDSU student who had skidded through a stop sign. Our car was twirled around on the ice, and we got hit again, this time by a car from the south. Luckily, all seat belts were fastened, and only our car was damaged.

An elderly couple came along and volunteered to take the girls on to school and their exams. I had to stay with the car, talk with the police, and see that the car got towed.

It would be a full day. Duane and I traded the damaged car for a new one midday, and that evening we hosted Shirley and Carl Menzies for dinner. Carl, who had helped form the 4-H club in Manhattan, was interviewing to head SDSU's animal science department.

The day ended well—the girls completed their midterm exams, I had a new car to drive, and Carl accepted the job, meaning the Menzies would be moving to Brookings.

The Dames' Club

The value of the student wives' groups that I had worked with at Iowa State prompted Mary Helen Hopponen, wife of the dean of pharmacy, and me to visit with longtime dean of women Vivian Volstorff about forming such a group at SDSU. (Mary Helen and her husband had arrived from the University of Kansas the same weekend Duane and I had arrived from Kansas State.) I described the Iowa State experience, and Mary Helen and I asked for Volstorff's endorsement. She was most enthusiastic and urged us to proceed.

The students' wives had their organization meeting, including election of officers, in Duane's and my campus home and named their group the Dames' Club. More than once in the months ahead, Duane would come home from a campus or out-state event to find members of the group still visiting in our living room or kitchen. The club was filling a need; I wonder and hope that, at this writing, fall of 2018, the group still exists or the need is otherwise being filled.

The organizing members of the SDSU Dames' Club, wives of students, in our campus home. (Reprinted with permission of the Brookings Register.)

Mary Helen and I were helpful to Dean Volstorff in another way. After hearing comments from a number of women students, we rather gently conveyed that the time was past for insisting on hats and white gloves for young women's receptions and teas.

Youth Council and Friends of the Library

Brookings mayor Orrin Juel and the city commission asked me to serve on a city youth council. According to a clipping from the *Brookings Register* I yet have, the council would "meet the third Sunday of every month at City Hall at 2 p.m." High school members of the council said they needed a hangout, and we saw the former fire station west of Main Street as a possibility. We, including Phil Hegg, Joe Farnham, and others of the council, cleaned out the station's truck stalls and painted the door yellow, prompting the students to choose the name, The Yellow Door.

We also opened a youth employment service (YES) on the second floor of city hall. As indicated in another clipping, it would be "open at 8 a.m. each day for the convenience of those with one-day only or part time jobs. Employers seeking youth employees are urged to call YES." Serving as a member of that youth council was a fascinating and rewarding experience.

Both our daughters had been avid readers from their preschool years in Ames. Diane, by then an eighth grader, encountered a problem in the Brookings library; she was not allowed to check out books from the adult section. Her experience may not have been the only reason, but several of us took it upon ourselves to form a "friends of the library" group, and I served as the first president. The friends' group was needed; feedback and a bit of pressure from users helped to open up what had been, in many ways, limiting constraints.

A Clothing Allowance

Nylon hose were in vogue, even for junior high girls, in the late 1960s, and almost-daily runs were costly. That prompted us to put each daughter on a monthly clothing allowance and purchase for each a portable sewing machine. They could decide how much they wanted to spend on hose. I do not recall the monthly allowance dollar amount, but I do recall it excluded heavy winter coats and boots.

Fortunately, there was an excellent fabric and pattern store in downtown Brookings, and both Diane and LuAnn became steady customers. Each developed extraordinary skill in both sewing and design. LuAnn entered a 4-H "Make It with Wool" competition with a winter coat and placed second in state competition, the judging done at Spearfish, and she also made a sport jacket for Duane. Both still make good use of their skills, making draperies, making or altering clothes, and, in the case of LuAnn, quilting.

In my free time I took advantage of knitting lessons and found knitting to be a hobby I enjoyed. For Christmas, I knitted ski sweaters for all four of our family.

Both our daughters also did well in high school debate, with many wins, and Diane participated in the national forensics tournament three years, placing second one year in extemporaneous competition.

We encouraged our daughters to get summer jobs. LuAnn worked for the Dracys at their bookstore in Aggieville, and Diane worked in the university admissions office.

Hosting

As in Manhattan, we had the pleasure of hosting a good many faculty, students, and others in our home and usually served "snowballs," comprised of whipped cream, coconut, crushed pineapple, and vanilla wafers. My snowballs became popular and almost expected when faculty received an invitation to the dean's house. For the snowballs, I give credit to Esther Stengel, the wife of one of Duane's Iowa State advisees, for the idea and to a Mrs. May, who ran a small eating facility on Brookings's East Highway 14, for the recipe. At least three times during our eight years in Brookings, we invited, in a series of open houses, all the college faculty. My calendar shows the first series, six evenings between April 11 and April 22, 1967, and mentions the snowballs. We also hosted an open house a couple of times when statewide extension staff were on campus for their annual conference.

It was almost routine that when a candidate from elsewhere for a department headship was on campus, we would invite all of that department faculty and their spouses to a reception at our home to meet and visit with the candidate and spouse. When we had arrived at SDSU, all fifteen department heads in the college were older than Duane, several close to retirement, so during our eight years at SDSU there were several such events.

Twentieth Anniversary of the Marshall Plan

An unexpected and surprising opportunity came in the fall of 1967, our second year at SDSU; Duane was one of fifty US citizens invited by the former West German government to come to Germany to help commemorate the twentieth anniversary of the post-WWII Marshall Plan and see some of its consequences. We never learned why Duane's name was on the list, but I was invited to join him for the two weeks. We would visit manufacturing facilities, farms, and ports in many sections of what was then the Federal Republic of Germany (referred to as West Germany) and including Berlin. Especially because of my German heritage, it was a fantastic experience.

The fifty were divided into five groups and scheduled in successive time periods. Our group, ten plus spouses, had gathered for departure at New York's Kennedy Airport, and we found it an interesting group, including a former congressional candidate from Indiana, a university regent from Michigan, a state Democratic chairman from Missouri, an attorney general of Montana, Los Angeles city councilman Tom Bradley, an attorney from Georgia, and radio personality "Cousin Brucie" from New York. Bradley would later, during our years at Kansas State, gain recognition as a successful LA mayor and potential presidential candidate and would accept an invitation to be one of our K-State Landon lecturers.

Our Marshall Plan group at Berlin's Brandenburg Gate. Behind me is Los Angeles city council member Tom Bradley. The two men standing nearer the camera are, on the left, our host, an assistant minister of finance for the Federal Republic, and Montana Attorney General Forrest Anderson, who later became Montana governor. Cousin Brucie is the man holding the camera.

Foreign Language

We had encouraged Diane and LuAnn to each take a foreign language in high school and had told them we would take them to the language's home country. They would have the responsibility of reading the traffic signs and making the arrangements for hotels and restaurants. Diane chose Spanish, LuAnn German. So the summer of 1970, following their junior and sophomore years, respectively, we saw considerable of Europe. We flew Icelandic Air to Luxembourg, drove a rented Fiat to a Wiesbaden bed-and-breakfast, and visited with friends from our years in Oklahoma. From there we drove to Hamburg and spent a weekend with my distant German relatives, the Kohnens.

Germany was yet divided, and we could drive to Berlin only via a checkpoint at Hanover and a corridor highway to a checkpoint at the edge of Berlin. Once in Berlin, we saw the contrast between the new and brightly lit Europa Shopping Mall versus, beyond Checkpoint Charlie, the drabness of East Berlin's business and cultural districts. After Berlin, it was through another corridor, checkpoints at each end, to Stuttgart and a feeling of freedom.

We found few available *zimmers* (rooms) near Stuttgart, but with her elementary German skills and persistence, LuAnn found us a pair in a small-town pub. The next day it was on to Geneva, Switzerland, where, yes, we all enjoyed iced tea (then an unknown in Germany) and an English-language movie.

From Geneva, we drove down the Rhône Valley of France to Nice, and three recollections are prominent—the Roman ruins in the city, the tiny hotel parking garage with our car wedged tightly, and a flat tire discovered the next morning. But the drive around the Mediterranean, across the Spanish border, and into Barcelona was enjoyable.

During our three days in Barcelona, Duane exchanged the troublesome Fiat for train tickets to Paris. Our small Paris hotel, in which Duane had spent a week earlier that spring for an international conference, was two blocks down a side street from the Arc de Triomphe. A visit to the Louvre, a city bus tour, a movie, and shopping gave us a good feel for Paris.

Then it was a short flight to London and a trip on the Underground to our hotel, with third-floor rooms that seemed squeezed in under a sloping roof. As in other cities, we started with a city tour, in this case on a double-decker bus. Such a tour gave us the basics, outlining the parameters of the city, and helped us identify specific sites or areas we wanted to visit in more detail. Of course, Buckingham Palace and the changing of the guard were high on our list.

As I look back, this may have been the most valuable of our many family travels. For Diane and LuAnn, especially, it introduced different cultures, menus, and traditions. It reminded all of us of the discomforts, tiredness, and frustrations of lengthy travel, in this case two weeks. It also built confidence in embarking on future international travel.

Duane and I suggest in jest that perhaps we overdid our daughters' travel experiences; we now have difficulty keeping track of their travels!

Ready for College

Soon our daughters would be off to college, Diane to Drake University in Des Moines to major in political science and LuAnn to the Morris campus of the University of Minnesota to prepare for admission to a school of physical therapy.

During Diane's second year at Drake, she arranged through Fairleigh Dickinson University in New Jersey to study abroad for a semester at Wroxton

College in England, the credits applicable at Drake. She took a part-time job in Drake's chemistry department office to earn money for the extra cost.

We had urged both our daughters to choose their own profession and then go to the best school they could get into. Diane's target, from early in life, was law. She chose Harvard for law school, earned her degree there in 1977, joined a large Kansas City firm, made partner, and then resigned to establish her own firm. She has had a highly successful career, largely focused on helping investors recover funds after one or another form of securities fraud.

LuAnn, having worked as a candy striper during high school, chose physical therapy (PT). While doing her pre-PT work at Minnesota's Morris campus, she checked out several highly recommended programs, including Saint Louis University. By that time we were moving to the University of Nebraska, which had a PT school on the Omaha campus (so there would be no out-of-state tuition). However, the school at the University of Minnesota appeared the strongest, so she enrolled and completed her degree there.

LuAnn gained many satisfactions from hands-on work, largely helping patients recover from orthopedic surgery, then moved to highly successful vice presidential roles with several therapist-providing firms in both the Southeast and Midwest, becoming responsible for both recruiting personnel and managing contracts in the range of health therapy. In time, though, she returned to her first love, hands-on therapy for individual patients. We still get compliments from some of her former patients.

We took advantage of Diane's spring semester break at Wroxton in 1973 for a week traveling with her through Wales, southern Ireland, and up to Hadrian's wall in Scotland. Our last stop was Shakespeare's home base, Stratford on Avon. We then dropped Diane back at Wroxton and headed to Heathrow Airport.

Before departing Brookings, we had learned that some SDSU education students were doing their practice teaching in one of the north London suburbs, so we stopped for a short visit with them on our way to Heathrow.

Inaugurations

Especially in a small-population state dependent on agriculture, such as South Dakota, the dean of agriculture is often called upon by state legislators, the governor, or members of Congress to be involved in key issues or events, whether state or federal and regardless of political party. Consequently, we drove to Pierre for the inauguration of a new governor, Richard Kneip, a Democrat, and flew to Washington, DC, for Republican Richard Nixon's second inauguration. In each case, the highlight for me was the inaugural ball. In Pierre the ball was in the Pierre High School gym; for Nixon's inauguration there were many ball locations and we were among those who danced at the Smithsonian Museum of Natural History.

Dinner and Dancing at the White House

Because agricultural groups had been visibly helpful in Nixon's reelection, he arranged a Salute to Agriculture Day in early spring that would climax with a dinner in the White House. Key agricultural leaders and spouses from across the country were invited. As Duane was chair of the US Deans of Agriculture that year, we were among the invitees. The day's agenda included behind-the-scenes presentations in the USDA's Jefferson Auditorium by Alexander Haig, assistant to the president, and Attorney General Ed Meese, then afternoon exhibits on the White House lawn. Other spouses and I had a luncheon at the Blair House, across the street from the White House.

The White House lawn exhibits ranged from genetically improved chickens, pigs, and sheep to a then-new International Harvester air-driven corn planter. By coincidence, several of the USDA scientists tending the animal exhibits were among Duane's longtime acquaintances and friends.

As to the evening dinner and dance, my immediate concern on learning of the invitation was, *What will I wear?* After shopping for a gown, to no avail, I decided to make my own. I found a pattern and some light-blue satin and made a long gown and coat. I was pleased with the outcome and was sure I would feel comfortable and confident at the dinner.

Modeling the gown I designed and made for dinner at the White House, spring of 1973. (Reprinted with permission of the Brookings Register.)

We had been unnerved, though, when we arrived in our Washington hotel the evening before the event, after a flight in from Brookings, to find that we had neglected to bring along the engraved dinner invitation! Would we be admitted to the White House and dinner without it? We called home, asked our daughters to put the invitation inside a bathrobe, pack it in a small suitcase, take the suitcase down to the Brookings airport, tell the agent we had forgotten one bag, and provide the name of our hotel. At four thirty the next afternoon, when we returned to our hotel from the White House lawn exhibits, the bag was lying on our bed! How wonderful it was to be living in a small midwestern town where people knew and helped each other!

As we entered the White House East Room receiving line to be greeted by President and Mrs. Nixon, we were each given a card with our table number, mine toward the west portion of the state dining room, Duane's along the east wall. Being among the first, as the receiving line was arranged alphabetically, I could greet my table partners as they arrived, among them Mrs. Bob Dole (the first Mrs. Dole, before Elizabeth), Senator Jack Miller of Iowa, and Secretary of Agriculture Cliff Hardin. Conversation was easy. Dole had been a congressman during our earlier time at K-State, Miller and I had mutual Iowa acquaintances, and Hardin had been chancellor of the University of Nebraska while we had lived in three adjacent states. After dinner and comments by the president, Glen Campbell entertained in the East Room, drinks and coffee were served in several of the smaller rooms, and, later, Duane and I danced in the White House foyer.

Throughout the evening, I was fully comfortable with my blue satin gown, and there was not another like it!

Reports of our White House visit brought an invitation from Jeanette Horn, our daughters' debate coach, to speak at the South Dakota state convention of Alpha Delta Kappa, an honorary organization for women speech educators. Though I had been a bit nervous about speaking to speech educators, I wore the blue satin dress. That gave me comfort, and the audience was most attentive.

Time for Parties

A series of couples' parties during our eight years in Brookings and its Methodist church gave us much fun. Several times during the year, two couples would plan a party and invite the others, often with some element of mystery, secrecy, or deception. Even the hosts might not be identified, and invitees sometimes could find the party location only by following a series of clues or by chance.

We once planned a hobo party with Peggy and Vernon Kirk. Through a Northwestern Railway friend, Vern arranged for a boxcar to be parked on a siding at the edge of downtown Aurora, a village a few miles east of Brookings. Invitations gave only the date and time, a Saturday evening, and said that each guest should dress as a hobo and should go to the bulletin board at Aurora's general store that evening for more instructions. In the meantime, we had gathered tin food cans, a cast-iron kettle, a tripod to hang it on, and the necessary ingredients for hobo stew.

Saturday afternoon we delivered bales of straw to the boxcar and, for skits we intended our guests to perform, hung a sheet as a stage curtain. A freight came along on the main track while we were working, the engineer leaning out to see what was going on. He spotted the iron kettle and, through the car door, the bales of straw, and he gave us a wave and a big smile.

A series of out-of-town cars stopped at Aurora's general store about seven o'clock that Saturday evening. Each driver checked the bulletin board and then sped on down along the railroad track. That did not go unnoticed among the natives. The town constable soon showed up to find out what was going on and had a good laugh.

Our time in Brookings was a wonderful eight years. I can't think of a friendlier place to live while raising our two daughters. We knew their friends and their friends' parents. And, for me, the foreign travel, my involvement with university and community issues, and exposure to the world of politics at both the state and national levels were fantastic experiences. My world became wider.

To Nebraska

In early 1974, we were again on the move. Duane had been offered a vice chancellor position at the University of Nebraska–Lincoln effective April 1. With both of our daughters in college, it was a good time to move; we would not be interrupting their school friendships.

We purchased a large split-level home in east Lincoln, at 600 Hazelwood Drive. Duane would have two offices, one on the East Campus, where most of his Institute of Agriculture and Natural Resources units were located, and another on the City Campus in downtown Lincoln. The latter ensured that he was, and was perceived as, part of the central university leadership team. Plus, one of his institute units, the Conservation and Survey Division, was on the downtown campus.

A Moving Adventure

Our late-March moving day, the day the van would deliver our furniture and we would drive the three hundred miles to Lincoln, was, in itself, an adventure. LuAnn, home from college, and I first stopped at an auto dealership in Sioux Falls to deliver our two-door Buick, which we were trading for two new cars, a four-door Buick Skylark and a two-door Honda hatchback. LuAnn would drive the Honda to Lincoln, and our dachshund, Tena, would be with me in the Skylark. Duane had left Brookings earlier that morning with our 1929 Model A Ford filled with potted plants, arriving in Sioux Falls in time for his last Norwest National Bank board meeting and meeting up with us at the dealership after.

At one o'clock, our planned departure time from Sioux Falls, the Skylark was not ready, so Duane and LuAnn departed. I left Sioux Falls an hour or so later and expected to catch up to them on the way, taking I-29 to Omaha and I-80 on to Lincoln. By near dark I was at the outskirts of Lincoln and had seen neither the Honda nor the Model A. Perhaps they had made better time than expected and would be at our new home and have the heat on.

However, when I pulled up to 600 Hazelwood Drive, the house was dark, and there was no Honda or Model A in sight! I did have a house key, so Tena and I were able to get into the house. What to do? I called Duane's parents; perhaps Duane had had trouble with the Model A and had called them. (This was before cell phones, and we had a standing agreement to call one of our parents if we were separated and needed to communicate.)

Duane had not called his parents, but soon he and LuAnn arrived, both in the Honda. He had had to stop off I-29 midway in western Iowa for generator adjustment, LuAnn following him, and I had passed them by. Later, in Omaha, darkness approaching and his headlights not working well, a generous gasoline station manager had let him leave the Model A in the station's service bay. He would retrieve it the next morning.

Life in a Residential Area

With our move from a campus home to the residential area of a larger city, my life would be different. Fortunately, we had great neighbors, including Mary and Lyle Hansen. Mary would be my neighborhood walking companion. Lyle, a research geologist, spent much of the summer in Greenland and much of the winter in Antarctica, pulling deep cores of ice, their content providing clues to global atmospheric events of earlier centuries. We were fascinated by his work, a different type of science from our acquaintance.

Years later, on a trip to New Zealand and Australia, we would visit the US base for this research, a facility at the Christchurch airport. When we mentioned Hansen to our facility host, he responded, "Lyle happens to be in town, just returned last night from Antarctica!" He contacted Lyle, who rushed to the base to visit and update us on his work.

Welcoming Activities

There were, of course, several Nebraska welcoming coffees and parties. Nebraskans, as South Dakotans and Kansans had been, were so kind and thoughtful.

Calendar excerpts best describe my "social" life our first weeks in Lincoln: April 2, Ceres Club (institute wives) to get acquainted; April 30, tea at governor's mansion; May 8, Faculty Women's Club and League of Women Voters; May 10, College of Agriculture graduation reception at the East Campus Library; May 12, Ceres Club at our home, 1:00 p.m.

We attended a nearby Presbyterian church, and I was invited to join Lincoln's CS Chapter of PEO, both opportunities to establish new friendships. My major social responsibility, however, was to prepare for and host, as at SDSU, Duane's institute faculty and spouses.

The institute was a new structure established by the state legislature and, with Duane new to the state, he was on the road many days meeting with industry and public groups related to the institute. It was not until October that we could set aside eight evenings for hosting, October 14–18, 21, 23, and 25. Because the institute's many programs also related to other parts of the campus, we included central campus administrators and deans of other colleges as well as several key state senators (Nebraska is a one-body, or unicameral, legislature, and all members are called senators) and industry people headquartered in Lincoln.

My Ride in a Police Car

My neighbors likely wondered what I had been up to when they saw the Lincoln Police drop me off at our home about five thirty on a Wednesday afternoon our first summer. I needed to explain. We had loaned our little Honda hatchback to LuAnn for her summer bookstore job in Brookings, and Duane had driven our Buick to Iowa at noon for an afternoon at the farm with his widowed father. I had only our 1929 Model A Ford to drive to a Ceres Club gathering across town.

All went well until my return. In heavy rush-hour traffic on Seventy-Second Street two miles from home, the Model A died, and I could not get it restarted.

A kind motorist pushed as I guided it off to the side of the road, and soon a police car pulled up behind. The officer, likely in his twenties, had no more familiarity with the workings of an antique than did I. I told him Duane would be back later in the evening and could retrieve the car. He put a red sticker on the windshield (to alert colleagues it was not abandoned) and offered me a ride home.

About nine thirty that evening I drove Duane over to Seventy-Second Street, he with a screwdriver (to check the switch wiring) and a box-end wrench (in case the starter engine was stuck). In a few minutes he had it running and followed me home.

Haying the Bridges

A highlight of our time in Nebraska was an invitation to the Forrest Lee ranch in Nebraska's Sand Hills, to help move cattle from a distant pasture to ranch headquarters. After a Sunday evening visit with the Lee family in their home, we were up early so Duane could dress for a daylong horseback ride and help move the cattle. Mr. Lee and I spread hay on the bridge floors along the route so the cattle would not be spooked by the rumble of the bridge planks; the cattle would eat their way across. (More detail of that day is in Duane's memoir *From Troublesome Creek.*)

Nebraska Football

With Nebraska's football prominence, steadily winning or close to winning the Big Eight Conference championship, we wore our "Big Red" for a full day of activity for every home game. There was usually a luncheon in the campus Union for a few senators and other guests, and we would help host guests in the president's and chancellor's box above the stadium and would usually attend one or two postgame events. A bonus was being part of the Sugar Bowl contingent, with other university officers and regents and spouses, for a few days in New Orleans.

Back to Kansas?

In early 1975, either January or February, Duane was invited to submit his résumé for the presidency of Kansas State. Though we had reservations about considering such a quick move, the opportunity and lure were tempting. Duane first interviewed with a faculty-student-alumni search committee at a Kansas City airport motel. Several weeks later, he and I were called to come interview with the Board of Regents, and a week after that Duane was in Topeka for the final interview.

Duane called that evening to tell me that he had been chosen, that I was to fly to Topeka early the next morning for a public announcement, and that there should be no response if media called our home. Duane's father was at our home, recuperating from cataract surgery, so good neighbor Mary Hansen agreed to look in on him while I drove to Omaha for my flight and spent a day in Topeka. We would be moving back to Kansas State on July 1. Our time in Lincoln would be short, just fifteen months.

* * * * *

Chapter 1 described my first year in the president's home. That year reinforced my earlier perceptions, especially from my interactions at South Dakota State and the University of Nebraska, that there are many bright stars in a university's orbit, not only faculty and students but also key support staff, political leaders, industry clientele, community leaders, and donors. And not to be overlooked but appreciated are faculty spouses and students' parents. Over the next ten years I would meet, host, and work alongside so many that deserve to be called stars. And there would be many university guests, each a star in his or her own right and own field. It would be ten busy, interesting, and rewarding years. I believe the next chapter's title is therefore appropriate.

CHAPTER 4

Walking with the Stars

Duane and I had made the judgment that we would limit ourselves to ten years in these presidential roles. Life in each of our earlier locations had been so enjoyable and rewarding, each providing new and different experiences. We could not see ourselves settling in for the duration. At the end of ten years, we would yet be in our mid-fifties, and there should be other new and rewarding experiences to have.

Duane's predecessor, Dr. McCain, had been president for twenty-five years, and one of Duane's mentors had warned him, "A long-time university dean or president is usually followed by a short-timer." Knowing the perils of the circumstance, Duane had privately told a few friends his goal was to "survive for six years and stay no longer than ten." Regardless of the number, we wanted our years in the president's home to have positive impact on the university, its faculty, and its students.

Our second year began with a busy schedule:

> Wednesday, August 18, 2:45–3:20 p.m.—coffee in our home for parents of new students.
>
> Monday, August 30, 7:00 p.m.—dinner for General Benedict, new Fort Riley commander. (The university offered night classes on the base for military families, and a good many also took courses on campus.)
>
> Tuesday, August 31, 6:30 p.m.—Chamber of Commerce dinner at country club for new faculty.

Wednesday, September 1, 5:30 p.m.—dinner at Pi Kappa Phi fraternity.

Thursday, September 2, 5:00 p.m.—social hour and dinner with Student Senate, Union Flint Hills Room.

Saturday, September 4, 5:00 p.m.—BBQ and reception at home of Alumni Director Dean Hess.

The following Saturday marked the start of the football season and was Parents' Day. We joined the members of Chimes, a women's honorary organization, for a luncheon with parents in the Union's Flint Hills Room and, after the game with Brigham Young, went to a buffet for Parents of the Year and other guests. At 8:00 p.m. Bob Hope gave a performance in Ahearn Field House. The next day, Sunday, we lunched at 12:45 with students in the Smith Scholarship House, attended a two o'clock tea for fraternity and sorority house mothers in the Union Bluemont Room, and between 5:00 and 8:00 p.m. visited the Activities Carnival in the Union, which was filled with booths and displays that student clubs and interest groups had set up to entice new students to get involved.

The next three days Duane was in southwestern Kansas, Garden City, Liberal, and Hugoton, for some citizen forums he had arranged, talks to service clubs, an experiment station field day, and visits to extension offices. Thursday night we were both in Topeka for a retirement dinner for Max Bickford, executive director of the Board of Regents, and Saturday night we attended a dinner in Springfield, Missouri, with area alumni.

So it went. Back on campus on Monday, September 20, at 7:30 p.m., it was fruit punch and cookies in our home for about thirty new faculty and spouses. We were at evening dinners the balance of the week, with Russian visitors at the country club, a sorority, the Alpha Chi Omega fraternity, and, on Friday night, the Union for Endowment Association trustees. Saturday was the Wake Forest football game, preceded by the endowment trustees meeting and lunch. At 8:00 p.m. was a piano recital in McCain Auditorium.

Manhattan Townspeople

Manhattan people had been so generous to us that we wanted to reciprocate with a bit of hospitality. We had hoped to do this our first year, but time just did not permit. Of course, many had been eager to see the updated president's home and, perhaps, how I had furnished it. So on Tuesday and Wednesday evenings, September 28 and 29, from 7:00 to 8:00 and 8:30 to 9:30, we greeted townspeople to an open house.

There also came an opportunity to let more of the university's statewide staff, those in county and area extension offices, know they were considered an important part of the university. On Monday, October 30, from 2:00 to 5:00 p.m., we served coffee in our home for statewide extension faculty attending their annual campus meeting.

Time Off to Celebrate Our Twenty-Fifth Anniversary

We spent a few weekends at our Iowa farm the first eighteen months of Duane's presidency, but our university commitments had precluded any extended time away. We therefore made plans to celebrate our twenty-fifth wedding anniversary with a ten-day trip to New Zealand and Australia after fall semester. We would depart after the Big Eight holiday basketball tournament and be back before the 1977 legislature was fully underway.

My memory of the experience is yet vivid, and I record here some detail of the travel. Though we covered much territory, the experience was a needed refreshment from the previous eighteen months.

After an overnight at Santa Barbara with Duane's sister and husband, Lorraine and John Rasmussen, we flew via San Francisco to Auckland, arriving midmorning New Year's Eve, and headed south in a rented car through lush, green-grass country, azaleas in full bloom. By the time we reached Rotorua, we were ready for a motel, dinner, and bed. However, the motel was hosting a New Year dining celebration, a Maori hangi, with meat and vegetables wrapped in leaves within muslin bags and roasted in the steaming "lava" pits. There was space for us, so we joined in, enjoying the meal and, especially, dancers in their native costumes. The distinguishing features of the dancing, unusual and initially shocking, were the bulging eyeballs, extended tongues, and associated facial expressions that some would consider grotesque. For the evening, with local and hotel guests, we were immersed in another culture.

We drove on past dairy farms and orchards and through small towns to the North Island's south-coast town of Wellington, expecting to take a scheduled ferry to the South Island. However, the ferry had in recent days closed its business. Disappointed, we turned in the car at the Wellington airport and flew to Christchurch.

Unfortunately, it was a Friday, and Christchurch, including theaters and businesses, had essentially shut down for the weekend. We walked the city parks, visited churches, purchased Sunday-evening food at a kiosk to eat in our hotel room, and awaited Monday, when we could hire a car for a drive to Mount Cook. Though what we saw of the South Island was attractive, cultivated flatland south of Christchurch and flocks of sheep grazing in the foothills, Mount Cook itself was shrouded in fog.

We were back early at the Christchurch airport for a flight to Melbourne and there had our visit with former Lincoln neighbor Lyle Hansen, just back from Antarctica, as described on earlier pages.

In Australia we drove by rented car from Melbourne to Canberra to Sydney, with intermediate stops that included spending a half day at a zoo/preserve, sitting in the bleachers at a rural cattle auction, watching an apricot packing operation from above the flow of harvested apricots, and receiving a bag of apricots from a generous and hospitable producer. Several times we stopped at a roadside market for a refreshing Australian "milkshake," a chilled blend of milk and coffee.

Whereas most nations' capitals had been established at or become population centers, Canberra had been planned in the early 1900s for the sole purpose of being the country's capital. Consequently, the focus of the city was government, not commerce. Any commerce—restaurants, hotels, and so on—existed to serve those who related to the central government.

Our car was low on gas, but we saw no convenient gasoline stations in the heart of the city. We did not fear, assuming we would find one on the outskirts of the city as we headed toward Sydney. Not so! The only exception to private homes along our major highway as we left Canberra was a welcome center. We were perhaps twenty kilometers out in open country when we were relieved to spot a gasoline station alongside the highway.

K-State in the Philippines

Our return from Australia was by way of the Philippines, scheduled so we could visit with and see the living and working conditions of three K-State faculty in the early stages of an Agency for International Development–financed project at Central Luzon State University north of Manila. We also visited the University of the Philippines south of Manila and there spent time with José "Pepe" Eusebio, Duane's one-time graduate student at Iowa State. Pepe showed us his swine-nutrition research facilities and, because his family operated a tailor shop near the university campus, presented me with a long tailor-made dress. More details of our time in the Philippines appear in Duane's book *Back to Troublesome Creek*.

While in the Philippines, I was able to find, while shopping, a large white lace tablecloth I needed for my Ethan Allen dining table and entertaining. It is a treasure that I continue to use.

Back on Campus

Back on campus in mid-January 1977, a full hosting schedule awaited:

Saturday, January 22, 4:30 p.m.—Wildcat Club, members and leaders of clubs across the state.

Thursday, January 27, 7:30 p.m.—League of Women Voters (which I had joined).

Sunday, January 30, evening—student PEO chapter meeting.

Tuesday, February 15, 5:15 p.m.—dinner for key leaders of the Kansas Senate. This event I recall most vividly. The group was large enough that the only way we could accommodate them all was in the basement. We put tablecloths on our Ping-Pong table and on a sheet of plywood atop the pool table. We served buffet style from our dining room table, and our guests had to negotiate the stairs.

I insert here that, though the Ethan Allen dining table we had brought with us worked well as a buffet or for coffee and tea service for receptions, it was inadequate and appeared rather lonesome in a dining room that should accommodate eighteen. After several make-do efforts to host other legislator or donor groups for dinner, the K-State Foundation would, in time, have available funds to purchase an adequate table. I am grateful to good friends Al and Ruth Hostetler and Barbara and Bob Wilson for bringing that about.

Monday and Tuesday, April 18 and 19, 7:00–8:00 p.m. and 8:30–9:30 p.m.—faculty open house (new faculty members and some who had been on leave the previous year).

Monday, May 16, 6:30 p.m.—dinner for state House and Senate appropriations committee members.

Summers were a time for alumni gatherings across the state, and our first major hosting that fall was a reception for Red Skelton.

Red Skelton

Though we enjoyed all our guests, Red Skelton was special. Invited to the campus for a Saturday-evening performance in Ahearn Field House in September 1977, he had chosen to come a few days early. He said he wanted to sit in on some of our theater and dance classes. Of course, he would share with those classes his talents and give them encouragement.

We arranged a Thursday-evening reception and invited a number of faculty, townspeople, and students, perhaps fifty to sixty. Skelton placed himself just inside our living room and, for the entire evening, not only shook hands with each one but also engaged each in conversation. All who left our home that evening felt they had had a close relationship to Red Skelton.

The next morning our doorbell rang, and there was Red Skelton with a potted red kalanchoe for me. I have made successive cuttings from that plant and have long enjoyed the red blossoms. One of Skelton's paintings hangs in our side entry and daily reminds me of this outstanding comedian and outstanding person.

The Governor and His Cigarette

K-State hosted the University of Kansas football team on Saturday, October 23, and for that major in-state rivalry, Duane and I hosted a 10:00 a.m. coffee for Governor Bob and Olivia Bennett plus any regent members and legislators who would be coming for the game. Of course I wanted it to be a special event, not the normal coffee and bars or cookies, so my student helper and I had made fruit pizza. During the event, she and another student handled the pizza and coffee, and Duane and I greeted people at the door.

An apparent chain-smoker, the governor used a short cigarette holder and was holding it in his left hand as he and Olivia entered and shook our hands. We said nothing at the time about our no-smoking policy in the house, but as the Bennetts moved on, we quietly agreed to each other, "It is now or never." The governor's driver was coming through the door, and Duane said to him, "We don't want to embarrass the governor, but we have a policy of no smoking in the house. There are some smokers on the porch."

The driver was quick. "No problem. That is what I am here for. I'll take care of it."

Nothing more was said during the coffee or as the group departed, and though we expected no negative result, we were a bit apprehensive.

Duane later reported that at the game halftime Bennett leaned over and said, "You know, you are one of Olivia's favorite people."

Duane was surprised. "Why is that?"

"Because you don't allow any smoking in the house!"

Christmas

The Christmas season was a delightful time to be in the president's home. A residence hall group, fraternity, or sorority would often come by to sing Christmas carols. We would step out onto the front entry to enjoy and to thank them. On one occasion the carolers invited us to join them, off to another site and, later, back to their dormitory for cookies and punch. It was another chance to visit with individual students and to hear their thoughts, concerns, and joys.

Duane and I being serenaded by the men of Phi Kappa Alpha fraternity on our thirty-fourth wedding anniversary, March 23, 1986.

Short on Student Housing

From time to time there appeared an unexpected need. The fall of 1979 K-State brought a larger-than-expected enrollment of new students, and not all could be accommodated in student housing. I called Director of Housing Tom Frith and suggested that if he could find some cots or bunk beds, there was space on the third floor of the president's home. Beds soon appeared, along with four young women. Among the nearly three thousand new students, there would be a few who, due to illness, homesickness, or other problems, would leave a vacancy early in the semester. These young women were with us about a month.

Graduation Ceremony in our Backyard

By 1980, the numbers of spring graduates would grow to the point that it would no longer be practical to hold the Saturday ceremony for all undergraduates in Ahearn Field House. There would be a university-wide ceremony midmorning for Duane to congratulate all graduates and their parents, award honorary doctorates, and perhaps introduce an invited speaker; each college would later host their own event, especially the handing out of diplomas, in a smaller venue. The College of Human Ecology asked if it could hold its ceremony on our back lawn. It was a great idea, and I readily agreed.

Unfortunately, a heavy rain began midday that Saturday, and the only option was across the street in the college's small auditorium. About two fifteen our phone rang, and the caller was an irate mother. "Why wasn't there enough room for my family?" She said she would be calling the regents and the governor! I could only listen, sympathize with her circumstance, and let her vent her understandable frustration.

Spring-semester commencement was a two-day event, usually a reception in our home Friday afternoon or evening for honorees, breakfast for the commencement party at the stadium football complex, and related events following the formal ceremonies.

Women's Clubs and Groups

Though designated honorary chairman of the K-State Faculty Women's Club, I was careful to limit my role to attending club meetings, supporting the club's elected leaders, and, of course, offering our home for any meetings or club functions. I was also invited to be an honorary member of the local Domestic Science Club. I yet receive the annual program of each group and often receive invitations to special events. Because of distance, I can only send a note of thanks and appreciation. The current leaders are so thoughtful!

One of several women's groups I hosted during the pre-Christmas season. (Reprinted with permission of the Manhattan Mercury.)

Mention of women's groups reminds me of a near social tragedy. An ecumenical church group had finished their tea and cookies in our living room and were attentive to a presentation by a local minister I had just introduced. Our little dachshund, Tena, who had apparently finished her afternoon nap, wandered into the living room. She was ready for her afternoon walk.

She scanned the group, looked over at me, then raised her back and let go with a number two. Fortunately, she was right in front of good friend Marion Larson, who had seen the process and had a paper napkin handy. Fortunately, the speaker was a good one; I don't think most of the group knew what had happened.

Free Time

Though hosting and entertaining took much of my time, there were other joys. I walked Tena around the campus at least twice each day, and the students we encountered often stopped to visit or to ask if they could pet her. For them it may have been a reminder of home, a brief interlude from their study-centered life.

Two or three times a week I would go midday to the university natatorium for a half hour or hour of lap swimming. It was so relaxing! And for a time I joined a rope-jumping class organized by some members of the faculty women's club.

The university marching band practiced on the grounds just east of the president's home, and on a rare afternoon that I was not committed, I could sit on the back steps and enjoy the band's lively music.

Focus on Fund-Raising

Duane had added a second staff member to what was to be renamed the K-State Foundation and was focusing on building membership in a President's Club, consisting of donors of $10,000 or more. As part of that effort, we began hosting an annual fall barbecue for club members in our backyard. For one such event, we had a pig roast. The pigs were roasted in the animal science meat lab, and before the serving, Moki Palachio, a native of Hawaii who, with his wife, June, was helping us, gave them a colorful Hawaiian blessing. (For more history on the foundation and fund-raising, see Duane's memoir of his presidency, *Two at a Time*.)

We had not, over the years, served alcoholic beverages in our home. We were comfortable with Kansas being a dry state and also with the philosophy once expressed by the first university president we had personally known, Oliver Willham at Oklahoma A&M (now OSU): "If alcohol is not allowed in our students' dormitories, we should not be serving it in the president's home." However, about the time we began hosting the President's Club barbecue on our back lawn, the Kansas legislature passed legislation allowing the serving of alcoholic beverages in the governor's and university presidents' homes. Times had changed. We became convinced that some of our President's Club members would feel our hosting less than adequate if we did not serve alcohol, so a cash bar was provided on the south edge of the lawn.

As membership in the President's Club grew, in the early 1980s, we added a spring dinner event, its purpose to highlight a program that needed private funding or to celebrate a newly remodeled or completed structure. The first was in the reading room of Farrell Library, with white tablecloths over the reading room tables and a string quartet playing in the room's tiny balcony.

The next year the dinner was in the rebuilt Nichols Hall. It had been an abandoned, burned-out hull when we had returned to the campus in 1975, and its rebuilding and restoration to accommodate a new theater in the round and other functions had been a decade-long effort. Duane and I were brought to the historic double doors in a horse-drawn carriage to greet our President's Club dinner guests in the foyer and hallways, and the evening climaxed with a student performance of *Brigadoon*.

As the President's Club grew even more, foundation staff arranged winter travel programs for club members, and it was intended that if our schedules would permit, Duane and I might accompany. For one of the club's first travels, to the Caribbean, Duane had to cancel because of budget meetings with the legislature. I was not about to cancel and enjoyed both the warmth of the Caribbean and the personal warmth of these wonderful people supporting the university. I think I shocked them, however, when the group was invited to snorkel and I stepped forward. They may have been as surprised as some students at the natatorium were when they found they were swimming next to the president's wife. I am glad I snorkeled; it was a great experience!

Shirley Hansen Acker

Community Involvement

At the invitation of one of my longtime friends, I became involved with the Manhattan Civic Theatre and for several years devoted some mornings to their ticket sales room and phone. The theater also needed funds, so Duane and I hosted a fund-raiser for the theater at the president's home. It was a beautiful evening, and we rolled our piano out onto the back deck so we could entertain our friends on the lawn.

We had joined the First United Presbyterian Church, downtown, and I wanted to play whatever role would be helpful. I especially enjoyed being a regular participant in the church's Care Group, visiting shut-ins. It paralleled the group I had helped organize in South Dakota. It may have been this interest that led to my being asked to join the advisory board of the Riley County home health effort.

Perhaps my most fascinating community experience was serving on the board of St. Mary's Hospital, owned by the Salina-based Catholic diocese. It was at a time of community-wide concern about supporting two hospitals and expressions there should be some form of consolidation or at least a joint working relationship. It was a contentious time. After much discussion and negotiation, the two boards developed a division of labor agreement, with the birthing activity to be in the newer St. Mary's.

However, the agreement was rejected by the diocese bishop. A solution to Manhattan's two-hospital concerns would have to come later.

United Way had been one of my most rewarding community involvements in earlier years, so I was glad to help in Manhattan when asked. And that led to being asked to serve on the planning committee for what was called the "low-rise," a senior citizens' center near downtown.

I also helped most years with the campus blood drive, sponsored or cosponsored by the Red Cross. My job was usually handing cups of orange juice to the donors after their blood draw. Taking in a bit of liquid is insurance; donors have been known to faint after a draw. I especially encouraged the juice to any of our three-hundred-pound football players; at only a hundred pounds, I would not have been of much help had one fainted.

Back to the Campus

As I scan through my calendars, I note several events or activities not mentioned earlier that bring back good and positive memories, including coffee for wives of Kansas bankers on February 28, 1980; a reception in our home for thirty honor students at 3:30 p.m. on June 3, 1980; a women's athletes picnic we hosted on the adjacent band practice field; a bridal shower for former neighbor girl Terry Shull on October 11, 1980; a groundbreaking for the Quinlan Gardens on November 9, 1980; and an evening serenade by Blue Key and Mortar Board members.

Early in our time in the presidency, we had members of FarmHouse fraternity over for coffee and cookies. (Duane was a FarmHouse member at Iowa State, and the K-State chapter members had helped move our furniture from the garage when the house renovation had been completed.)

Certain campus events could be preceded or followed with a visit to the president's home. One not mentioned earlier was a dessert for Regent Elmer Jackson, a Kansas City, Kansas, attorney, after he had spent a half day on the campus to see how a land-grant university functioned. We used the dessert to acquaint him with K-State's Agency for International Development–financed project in Nigeria.

We had several state legislators at the house for coffee after a Christmas concert in McCain Auditorium. On March 23, our wedding anniversary, we had a coffee event for state legislators and students. The legislators had come to campus to see building needs and visit with students.

On several occasions I hosted a coffee for wives of legislators. I always tried to have a small memento for each, so I was careful to have a list of their names and the total number. After the coffee, I might find myself leading a bus or walking tour of the campus. I was proud of the campus, composed of virtually all limestone buildings, and enjoyed showing it to visitors.

About every two years, the Board of Regents would hold their two-day monthly meeting on the K-State campus, and that would usually include at least a coffee, perhaps a luncheon or dinner, in our home.

Especially during the summer, it was not uncommon for a state convention or national scientific meeting to be held on campus. On our back lawn we hosted the American Society of Animal Science and the American Society of Agricultural Engineers for barbecues. We also hosted the American

Association of University Women, PEO, and the wives of Kansas bankers in Manhattan for their state convention.

Another near tragedy occurred the morning after the American Society of Animal Science barbecue in our backyard. As South Dakota friend LaRayne Wahlstrom and I were having coffee in the kitchen, we heard a gust of wind, the cracking of some tree branches, and then a crash. A thirty-five-foot ash in the center of the barbecue site had uprooted and fallen.

I have likely forgotten many groups, but I must mention the Manhattan Book Club, which included so many good friends, and the Faculty Women's Club Style Show. For the latter, I modeled a green velvet gown loaned by one of the members. After the show, she suggested if fit me so well that I should keep it, and she generously gave it to me.

* * * * *

I record these events and groups not only to give the reader a glimpse of what may go on in a university president's campus home but also because they remind me of many satisfactions I had as first lady of a major university. Yes, there was work, and there were expectations to be fulfilled, but these were masked by the appreciation we saw as longtime or new faculty, or other guests, came through the door for their first visit. These memories and satisfactions remain.

I believe that every significant donor to K-State during our time—and many later donors—had been in our home for a reception, dinner, or other event.

I cannot leave these recollections without emphasizing my appreciation for our student helpers, those who occupied the maid's quarters as modest compensation for their generous help, as well as other students, faculty wives, and guests who pitched in from time to time. I could not have hosted these events without them.

In addition to Marilyn Funk and June and Moki Palachio, mentioned earlier, there were Heather Spence and, our last year, Paul and Sharon Geist. The Geists were newly married and spent their honeymoon year helping us. At this writing, their two daughters have already graduated from Kansas State.

All were outstanding help and a joy to work with. Moki Palachio, especially, gave us some laughs. I think he had been an entertainer in his younger days and, having married late in life a woman pursuing a graduate degree on a tight budget, was challenged in this new role of helping with household maintenance. I had to teach him how to dust, explaining that he should hold a dust cloth in one hand and furniture oil in the other. But he was always willing. He even volunteered to paint our tiny entry closet, but I had to laugh when I spotted him sitting on a chair as he painted.

I thank the K-State Union staff, who catered the backyard barbecues for the President's Club and convention groups. I am also grateful to the animal science meat lab staff, who roasted the pigs for some of the barbecues.

K-State was fortunate to have an outstanding music faculty, and they were always available to help, to add musical color, support, and background for university and foundation events. Their strength also helped attract well-known artists to the campus. Duane and I enjoyed the McCain Artist Series, largely guest musicians. Most memorable among those visitors were violinist Itzhak Perlman in 1981, cellist Yo-Yo Ma, and the Vienna Boys' Choir in 1984.

Beyond the Campus

Not every university function or responsibility was on campus. It was important that we represent K-State each fall at the American Royal's Kansas Night and at one or more legislator's dinners sponsored by the agriculture or business community in Topeka in February or March. Several winters we joined alumni staff for a series of alumni events, to places like Denver, Sun City, Los Angeles, and San Francisco. On one occasion, Duane had to interrupt the trip to get back to an appropriation committee hearing, so I went on with the group for a presentation in Portland, Oregon.

To further advance private fund-raising with alumni and university friends, the K-State Foundation encouraged key people in several communities to host events in their homes or local facilities. More times than I can specifically recall, we drove or flew to Phillipsburg, Hays, Wichita, or even Hastings, Nebraska, or Oklahoma City and Tulsa. I had become accustomed to flying in light aircraft during our years in South Dakota but never grew totally comfortable in the lightning, rain, or hail we would sometimes encounter on a late-night return flight.

Shirley Hansen Acker

My Chance to Paint

From my early school days, I had been interested in art, and I had purchased a home study course while in high school. With longtime friend Marian Larson, who had been a good friend since 1962 when we had both arrived for the first time at K-State, and new friend Wy Johnson, we asked K-State art professor Oscar Larmer if he would help us with watercolors. He agreed to and suggested we go to the Tuttle Creek dam area. After three afternoons under his guidance, we each had a Kansas scene in which we could take some pride and satisfaction. We appreciated Larmer's skills and patience.

After Larmer's instructions on the basics, Wy and I, bit by the fun of painting, often drove out into the Flint Hills areas to paint, and she did some especially expressive landscapes. It was great fun and provided enjoyable afternoons of friendship.

I enrolled in an online music-appreciation course taught by professor and former Oregon Lane neighbor Paul Shull. His course was excellent. It broadened my understanding of music and helped me appreciate more the features and qualities of good music. Paul, who had been director of K-State bands in earlier years, was then focused more on teaching cornet and other wind instruments as well as the music-appreciation course. His wife, Joan, was a talented organist, and she remains a dear friend. We enjoy periodic phone visits, and I keep track of the Shulls' children, Mike, Terry, and Kevin, and their families.

Konza Prairie

Early in our time at K-State, Nature Conservancy, a national group dedicated to preserving natural habitat, purchased the several-thousand-acre Dewey Ranch south of Manhattan, with the understanding it would be managed and used by K-State faculty for research and demonstration in managing open grassland prairie (as well as ensuring habitat preservation). Being in the heart of the Kansas Flint Hills and representative of the vast Hills area, it was christened Konza Prairie. I recall two especially fascinating events at the ranch. The first was a student barn dance in the upper (hayloft) level of the ranch's massive stone barn.

Dancing at a FarmHouse fraternity party in the hayloft in Konza Prairie's massive stone barn. It had been more than a decade since Duane and I had square-danced, but we soon caught the cadence and joined in.

The second was a spring burn demonstration. Those driving I-70 through the Flint Hills on a spring night are likely to see lines of fire across the hills. Every few years, in early spring, Flint Hills ranchers burn off dead forage (and any invading trees or shrubs). A few weeks after the burn, a fresh, bright green carpet begins to show.

Most impressive is the rapid combustion of this dry grass. The fire needs to be set when there is little or no wind, and, most important, it must be started so that the fire line will progress toward any wind.

At this writing, October 2018, many California homes and businesses have been destroyed by record fires, with early-summer rains having caused dry and dense forage and with strong winds whipping the fire. Recalling the rapid combustion of dry grass and resulting intense heat in that Konza Prairie demonstration, I fully understand the pace and intensity of those California fires.

Guest Lecturers

George H. W. Bush, then vice president, came to K-State to give a Landon Lecture. I greeted him and his wife at the Manhattan airport, and they invited me to ride with them to the campus. I did not dream at the time that Duane and I would later be living in DC and I would be riding the Metro to the Volunteer Office in the Old Executive Office Building, there addressing cards and answering the White House phone for, first, President Ronald Reagan and, then, President George H. W. Bush.

Shirley Temple Black was also a great guest to the campus. She had accepted an invitation to be a Landon lecturer. The invitation was not because of her early-age acting career but because of her later roles as US representative to the United Nations and US ambassador to Ghana. During a walking tour of the campus, she asked me, "How long have you been a Shirley?" Yes, I was a bit younger than she.

Another of the Landon lecturers was Los Angeles mayor Tom Bradley. His lecture was special for Duane and me because the three of us had become acquainted years earlier as guests of the former West German government to help celebrate the twentieth anniversary of the Marshall Plan. Bradley stayed overnight in our home prior to the day of his lecture, and we had time to reminisce. Readers who have had flights to Hawaii or Southeast Asia scheduled through Los Angeles have likely walked through the Tom Bradley International Terminal.

K-State in Africa

During our earlier time in Manhattan, K-State began helping Ahmadu Bello University (ABU) in Zaria, Nigeria, develop colleges of agriculture and veterinary medicine, and I met some of the Nigerians who were earning degrees at K-State. By 1977, the project was ending, and we flew to Nigeria to help ABU celebrate what had been accomplished. Since 1963, about seventy-five K-State faculty had worked in this effort, most serving there two or more years.

In the Lagos airport terminal, after deplaning, we quickly learned what it is to be a minority, in this case the only whites in a sea of blacks.

En route to Zaria from Lagos we had a day at the International Institute of Tropical Agriculture in Ibadan, where the focus was on cassava, the major carbohydrate staple in many tropical areas, and rice, an important food in the lowlands of West Africa.

At ABU we were cohosted by Dr. Stanley Dennis, K-State's last remaining faculty member at ABU, and his wife. Dennis was then dean of the faculty and head of the Department of Veterinary Pathology and would leave for Manhattan July 1.

Duane was later asked to visit another Nigerian university, the University of Benin, to review and offer any advice on its agricultural college and research program. By then, K-State had several staff in Botswana helping develop that country's agricultural research, and we could visit both locations in one trip.

As with our experiences in other developing countries, the graciousness and hospitality of our University of Benin hosts seemed without limit. However, our drive back to the Lagos airport, with a graduate student as our chauffeur, was less than relaxing. The speedometer fluctuated between 120 and 150 kilometers per hour (70 to 90 miles per hour) all the way. Our nervousness was not abated by the dozens of wrecked and burned-out vehicles that dotted the road right-of-way.

Perhaps as vivid in my memory is the sight of seven- to nine-year-old children walking early morning alongside the road, obviously on their way to school and some balancing a chair or small desk on their head. Our hosts had told us that many rural schools were ill equipped.

We stopped off for a weekend in Nairobi, Kenya, and a two-day safari at Governors' Camp, about a hundred miles outside Nairobi. As we deplaned at the camp airstrip, waiting to board were good friends Ernie and Betty Mader. Ernie, a professor of agronomy, had been on an assignment in East Africa, and they had taken in Governors' Camp on their way back to Manhattan.

Snapshots taken during early-morning, mid-day, and late afternoon open-top Land Rover rides on Kenya's Serengeti Plain. Clockwise from the upper left: at our quarters, elephants, a wildebeest, and zebras.

From our faculty headquarters at Gaborone, Botswana, we traveled with K-State's Jim Jorns to several villages where village elders were conducting town meetings. Botswana extension staff were presenting education opportunities; the village elders' concurrence would give credibility for them to proceed with their work.

We also visited two farms. In each case the husband was away tending the family cattle on open range, and the wife and children were tending the grain sorghum crop. When harvested, the grain, the family's food staple, would be stored in large crockery vessels and a small round metal bin.

There was a bonus to our several days in Botswana. Several of Duane's former SDSU faculty were also in Gaborone, working under an Agency for International Development contract with the country's two-year agricultural college just down the road from where the K-State faculty was headquartered. All, including spouses, were friends, and we were invited to stay with Duane and Marilyn Everett, members of a four-couple bridge group we had been part of in Brookings.

To China with People to People

Retired extension specialist Eleanor Anderson invited me to help her lead a People to People group of women from the US to China in the summer of 1980. I would pay my own way, of course, and I believe that was the case for Anderson. It would be a rich experience for each of us. It had only been in 1972 that President Richard Nixon had broken the several-decade diplomatic barrier between China and the US.

We had a direct but long flight from San Francisco to Hong Kong, then yet a British protectorate but the major entrée into China. During our two days in Hong Kong, scheduled so we could rest and adjust to the time change, we visited a day care facility for about 120 children aged two to five years and a pottery factory. In the latter were many artists who painted designs on pottery, then fixed the pigment by firing. It was similar to what I would be doing two decades later.

From Hong Kong it was by train to Canton and then to Nanning, a southern city where we visited a minority college for girls, the Hwange Institute for Nationals. Each of our group was assigned a student with whom we would spend the afternoon, visiting classrooms and college facilities. That gave each student, then studying English, an opportunity to converse in the language, and I was impressed by my partner's ability. At the end of the afternoon my partner asked if she could come to the United States and stay with me, but that, of course, was not to be.

It was then on toward Kunming and a zoo with many panda bears, for which China is well known. In Kunming, bicycles were everywhere. There were few cars, and though it was considered a relatively rural city, throngs of people filled the streets. Bicycles were not only for transporting people, from one to even a family, the wife and one child behind the rider and another on the handlebars. A biker might be delivering bags of groceries, straddling a bundle of lumber, or even balancing newly manufactured baskets, stacked ten or twenty high.

This southern part of China was then little industrialized, and there was yet much open country, far different from the smog of the northern cities we would later visit. We found our hotel at Kunming full, so we were taken by jeeps to the Stone Forest, or Shilin, for our overnight stay at the Grand Forest Lodge in an area of tall limestone spires, believed to be more than 270 million years old. This proved to be a bonus. The evening was topped off by young dancing girls in their colorful native dancing costumes, beautifully embroidered skirts and trousers. It was a highlight of our total China visit.

The next day, back in Kunming, we visited the three-hundred-bed Kunming Municipal Hospital, crowded, with eight beds to a room. The hospital included doctors' offices and a pharmacy. We watched the dispensing of pharmaceutical items, including the weighing of herbal leaves. Acupuncture was described to us as a common treatment for as many as two hundred medical problems or maladies.

On the tarmac at Beijing, China, 1980, while helping lead a People to People group.

We then flew to Beijing, established by the Communist government as the capital of China in 1949, and stayed in a hotel that was part of a multi-building complex some distance from central Beijing. Because my roommate was elderly and needed more time to start the day, I would rise and dress early, then leave the hotel to walk the grounds and the streets. Men and women, usually in small groups, would be doing their morning exercises. Being blonde, I seemed to be an attraction. Some would stand and stare at my blonde hair. Some would walk all the way around me, looking at my hair from all directions. All seemed happy, conveying a friendly greeting by a nod of the head or a smile.

The days were filled with Tiananmen Square, the Forbidden City, the Summer Palace, and the city zoo and its many pandas.

We also drove to the country, visiting a farming commune and, of course, the Great Wall, which I walked some distance. Back in the city we had a brief tour of a hospital for the people. The patients were yet in street clothes, and family members brought their food.

Eighteen years later, Duane and I would be in China as part of an Iowa State University lecture group. As we arrived and walked into our scheduled Beijing hotel, I would have the sensation of *I've been here before!* Yes, though the grounds were more neatly maintained and the hotel rooms had been updated, it was the same hotel that had been my Beijing headquarters in 1980. Other changes in China—thoroughfares packed with autos; tall, modern buildings; construction cranes everywhere; McDonalds; and other "American" features—were awesome.

Before we left Manhattan, I had invited eight Chinese students at K-State, all from universities or research institutes in the Beijing area, to our home for dinner and asked each to write a letter to his spouse yet in China. I would, with their help in making meeting arrangements, deliver their letters. Arrangements were made for our group to meet and host these eight wives at a Peking duck restaurant in central Beijing. It was a fantastic experience—emotional and rewarding. I do not believe any of these women had been in such a nice restaurant before. We then asked each to write a note to her husband, and I would deliver them back in Manhattan. For them, the experience was wondrous; for me, it was memorable.

There is an interesting side matter to note here. One of the students had brought along to our home a 1979 *World Book Encyclopedia* volume that contained a section on agriculture authored by Duane. He and his fellow graduate students were far more impressed with Duane's writing appearing in an encyclopedia than his being president of K-State; such illustrates the power and significance of the written word.

Now Grandchildren

Over the 1984 Christmas vacation, our family, including our daughters and their husbands, were to be together several days in Florida. Our time on the beach was interrupted by the unexpected birth in Fort Myers of our twin grandsons, Eric and Clay, to Diane and her husband, Terry. Their birth was premature, and the two weighed but one pound, thirteen ounces and one pound, eleven and a half ounces. It meant their survival was touch and go. However, they had awesome attention and care by the neonatal physicians and nurses, and all turned out well. At this writing, November, 2018, both are enjoying their work, Eric in Iowa City and Clay in Kansas City. Clay earned his degree from William Jewell in Liberty, Missouri, and Eric from the University of Iowa. (In 1998, at age 13, Clay had been diagnosed with a rare form of leukemia/lymphoma and had become a volunteer research subject with the National Cancer Institute, National Institutes of Health, Bethesda, MD. Thanks to NCI treatment, he was in remission for twenty years. After this manuscript had been edited for production, Clay's symptoms reappeared, available research drugs were ineffective, and he died June 17, 2019.)

* * * * *

Our limit of ten years in the presidency extended to eleven. At that point, reflecting Duane's interest in global agriculture, he accepted a position as director of food and agriculture for the US Agency for International Development (AID) in Washington, DC.

As we prepared to leave K-State, we were overwhelmed by the expressions of appreciation and "Godspeed." The climactic event was a generous reception and dinner hosted largely by Manhattan area leaders but attended by many from across the state.

But there was one more thing I wanted to do.

Cookies from Big Mama

For what seemed to be a steady flow of events at our home during the eleven years, physical plant staff always had the shrubs trimmed or the drives and walks cleared of snow. And they were quick to respond whenever there was a problem with the heating system or otherwise. They were clearly among my stars. On several occasions I had told one of the workers that their little service vehicle looked like fun and that I would like to ride in it sometime. But I had never had the chance.

I called the physical plant shop and asked if one of the staff would drive their service vehicle down to the house. I had made some cookies for them and wanted a ride up to the shop to join them for coffee.

I had earned the nickname "Big Mama," likely due to my size, 4' 11" and barely one hundred pounds. When a worker was heading to 100 Wilson Court, he might say, "We'll get that done for Big Mama." I was not supposed to know about the nickname but had learned of it through a student helper and appreciated the endearing humor.

It took a lot of restraint on my part to resist putting a note on the cookie tray that said, "With appreciation, from Big Mama."

CHAPTER 5

On the Potomac

Our move to the DC area, after growing up in Iowa and living in five midwestern university towns, would bring a significant life change. We had rented a three-bedroom colonial in a western suburb, Vienna, Virginia. The house was about a mile from the west end of the then new Metro Orange Line, and Duane would walk to the Metro station, then ride a half hour to his AID office overlooking the Potomac River.

At a dinner party a few months after our arrival in the DC area, Nollie Bentley, whose husband had preceded Duane as dean at SDSU and was by then an assistant secretary in USDA, asked if I would be interested in working in the White House Volunteer Office. I jumped at the chance and was soon riding the Metro three or more days a week to the Farragut West station in downtown Washington. From there it was a three-block walk south to the Executive Office Building (EOB), a few steps from the White House.

The EOB was ornate, of French Second Empire architecture, and had been built over seventeen years, 1871–1888, to house the Departments of State, War, and Navy and the White House stables. The Volunteer Office was on the ground floor; the Office of Management and Budget (OMB), the vice president's office, and other offices of the White House and executive branch occupied the balance of the building. As with other White House staff, I checked in through security each morning and soon knew and was known by the security staff.

Shirley Hansen Acker

The Volunteer Office

The major task each day for the twenty or so volunteers was to address greeting and congratulatory cards for the president, generally for a fiftieth or more wedding anniversary, over-eighty birthday, Eagle Scout achievement, or other event.

These cards would be treasured by the recipients, so we wanted them to be impressive in all respects. An office colleague, Betsy Raposa, and I therefore took Saturday-morning calligraphy lessons from the Smithsonian calligrapher. We could then make even the envelope addresses impressive.

Among the calligraphy forms, my choice was copperplate, which requires unique pen points and ink. I so enjoyed doing copperplate that, especially during Christmas card season, I would take home envelopes and a list to do at night and on weekends. Occasionally we were also asked to letter a scroll or certificate for a departing White House official.

With coworker Muriel Johnsrud at work in the White House Volunteer Office. Note the many boxes of cards and envelopes behind us.

Duane and I were asked to help greet guests at one of President and Mrs. Reagan's pre-Christmas Sunday receptions, this one for military personnel in the DC area and their spouses. Christmas cookies, breads, and cakes, along with coffee, tea, and punch, were served. We had earlier addressed Christmas cards for President and Mrs. Reagan to governors, members of Congress, political supporters, and heads of state, and we volunteers had been invited as a group to view the White House Christmas decorations.

Jamie Wyeth had been commissioned to paint the scene for the Reagans' card that year. This was of special interest to me; Duane and I had recently toured the Wyeth Museum in southeastern Pennsylvania and had learned of the talents of several Wyeth generations.

We volunteers also responded to other needs. I often helped answer "the White House phone." Several instruments were employed to handle the call volume, with each caller expressing concern or giving advice to the president. Concerns ranged from military retirement checks not arriving to the cruelty of putting shoes on racehorses, whatever they wanted the president to hear and perhaps do something about.

We made a record of each call, noting the name and address of the caller and the question or subject so White House staff could have a reading of public concerns and, in some cases, refer the caller's issue to the appropriate executive department or agency.

Our office once received a request for immediate help in the White House travel office. I quickly volunteered, excited to see more of what went on in the White House.

In the West Wing of the White House, perhaps the day I was
called on to help in the White House travel office.

We also served as greeters or as part of the welcoming crowd on the White House lawn for visiting heads of state. Each of us was given a small flag of the visitor's country, and a military band played the visitor's national anthem. We then heard comments by the visitor. Being short, I was usually near the front of the "crowd."

Hosting?

Did I miss the hosting and the university setting? Had it not been for my work in the White House Volunteer Office, yes, I would have missed it. In contrast to universities where we had served, the largest host city being Lincoln, Nebraska, federal agencies exist in a large metropolitan area, both within the District of Columbia (DC) and adjacent Virginia and Maryland suburbs. Duane's staff were in several DC locations, as well as around the world. Further, the homes of those stationed in DC were geographically scattered. For a unit head to host staff and spouses in their home was not a traditional part of the scene.

Our home on Edgelea Lane in Vienna, Virginia, about a mile from the then west end of the Metro's Orange Line.

However, having seen the value of staff and spouses knowing each other and being acknowledged with an invitation to the home of their unit head and spouse, Duane and I could not dismiss the thought. We set aside a Saturday morning, sent invitations to all of Duane's DC staff and a few others with whom he worked closely, and provided directions to our home in Vienna.

We were overwhelmed by both the number that came and the friendship-renewal and new-friendship conversations in our living room and at the coffee-and-cookie table. Two couples had served in Peru at the same time years earlier, but their assignments since had precluded continued friendship. Some had worked together closely for years but not met the others' spouses. Perhaps they had unknowingly yearned for such an opportunity.

Again to Governors' Camp

Duane was scheduled to visit several AID efforts in Africa the following March, and this was my chance (as in university years, at our personal expense) for another visit to Kenya's Governors' Camp. My sister Norma Jean joined me, and she and I flew first to Hamburg, Germany, to visit our Kohnen relatives before meeting Duane in Kenya. The Kohnens were generous hosts and drove Norma Jean and me to our ancestral home, Bredstedt, near the Danish border, and to visits with more relatives.

Our flight to Kenya would depart from Frankfurt, so we rented a car in Hamburg and headed south on the autobahn, Norma Jean navigating and I driving. With drivers exceeding one hundred kilometers per hour and blinking their lights to pass, driving the autobahn was far different from the interstates of Kansas or Iowa. And it was far from my anticipations when learning to drive in the Acker pasture, a Jeep in low range.

Norma Jean carried information about a titled gentleman whom she had met during his visit to southern Missouri and who had invited her to sometime visit his Greifenstein Castle (Castle of the Bells). It was on our route to Frankfurt, and so we accepted his invitation. The day happened to be his fiftieth birthday. He was in the midst of preparing to host a party, but he was a gracious host, and we sampled some his party preparations. Then it was on to Frankfurt and our flight to Nairobi.

Our Nairobi airport welcome was a bit unnerving for Norma Jean. Foreign travel was a new experience for her, and her nervousness was evident. Customs staff took her to a private room to partially unrobe, to check for any currency she might be bringing into the country.

Duane would have three days in Nairobi reviewing international agricultural research centers and AID project headquarters, so Norma Jean and I flew out to

Governors' Camp for two days and nights. We had a two-person tent for sleeping and a smaller toilet tent adjacent. While in the toilet tent our first morning, Norma Jean heard the heavy, shrill scream of an elephant just outside. Apparently he had been scavenging for thrown-away lettuce at the nearby kitchen tent and was being chased away. She peeked out through the tent opening to find that the elephant was headed her way. Fortunately, the elephant turned and headed for open country. Norma Jean had had her thrill for the day.

Late morning, late afternoon, and just after sunrise the next morning, we would board an open-top Land Rover for drives over the Serengeti plain to watch the wildebeests, giraffes, elephants, lions, and other creatures. In the evening, from our outdoor cocktail hour gathering near the dining tent, we watched giant hippos wading across a nearby creek.

Later, departing from Nairobi, we joined Duane and his AID staff hosts in a six-passenger van to view a series of food-for-work and other AID projects plus Edgerton College, which University of Illinois staff were helping develop.

Back to the Volunteer Office

For the Saturday-morning Easter egg hunt, in a fenced-off area of the White House lawn, virtually all the volunteers would be helping. My job was to admit children in small groups of five or more, reminding each that he or she should pick up only one egg. Of course, there was a rare mother who insisted on accompanying her child and could not resist the temptation to pick up an egg or two for her pocket or purse.

My calendar reminds me that on the evening of October 7, 1987, we joined other guests of Duane's longtime friend and US Trade Representative Clayton Yeutter and his wife for a cruise on the *Sequoia*, the president's yacht. A week later I was on the White House lawn for the welcoming ceremony for El Salvador president Duarte. That was of special interest to me because a few years earlier we had hosted Duarte for a Landon Lecture at K-State. As Duarte was being introduced, I happened to be standing near the photographers' elevated platform. A photographer, I think Pete Souza, who had been a graduate student at K-State during our time, recognized me and my plight and helped me up onto the platform so I would have a better view. He later sent me some of the photos he had taken. Sometimes it pays to be short.

When addressing a card to the leader of a country I had visited—the Philippines, Australia, New Zealand, the Federal Republic of Germany, Nigeria, or Botswana, for example—or to a leader that had visited Kansas State during our time, such as from Rhodesia, I would feel a special thrill.

Friendship is sharing . . .
the laughter of happiness,
the frowns of concerns,
the smiles of success,
the sadness of disappointment.

Sharing . . .
builds a stronger
friendship filled with love.
Your friend
Shirley Acker

I so enjoyed calligraphy that on the days I was not at work in the White House Volunteer Office I might do my own thing.

Not only did I receive much satisfaction from the work, but the nearly six years I was in the White House Volunteer Office would be among the more interesting years of my life. And our work was appreciated, as indicated by repeated expressions by both the Reagans and Bushes. One gesture of appreciation, for example, was an invitation for Raposa and me to the Bushes' presidential suite in the Kennedy Center for an afternoon musical.

To Central American Countries

A few days after that Duarte ceremony, Duane, LuAnn, and I flew to Jamaica and from there to Guatemala and Honduras. Jamaica would be the site of a conference beginning on Monday for AID agricultural staff stationed in Latin America. We arrived on Saturday and hired a car and driver to circumvent the island.

Conference afternoons were devoted to site visits, to both AID projects and private-sector enterprises, and LuAnn and I could join the group. We saw irrigation projects; flowers grown for export, largely to the United

States; and livestock and poultry production. We were impressed by the productivity of this small island and the many business relationships to the US and Europe.

A few days later, in Guatemala City, we got a firsthand look at an AID food-for-work project, with teams of low-income community residents digging trenches and installing sewer pipe. Residents, both men and women, worked in morning and afternoon shifts, six hours each, and each team received three pounds of US rice, two and a half pounds of corn, and two pounds of beans per cubic meter of earth moved. These were surplus US commodities sent to Guatemala as part of our food aid program. A portion of the food had been sold to finance purchase of the sewer pipe, the city had designed the system, and the residents were receiving needed food for doing the work. CARE, a private voluntary organization, was handling the food distribution and supervising the work.

Local residents digging trenches for installation of sewer lines in the Kingston District of Guatemala City, each worker team paid with rice, corn, and beans from the US food aid program.

Working our way through a community of makeshift homes put together by Guatemalan families seeking employment and a better life in Guatemala City.

As soon as the sewer project was finished, these residents would be digging trenches and installing water lines to serve their homes, again being paid in food.

Our Guatemala hosts, AID and CARE staff, had the weekend off, so we flew to Santa Elena in northeastern Guatemala and then drove thirty minutes by taxi to Tikal National Park. We hired a young American student for a four-hour guided tour of Mayan ruins, visiting the ceremonial, athletic, educational, business, and residential structures of a civilization that had existed from 400 BC to AD 700. The civilization had dissipated in time and the structures abandoned, then rediscovered in the 1800s, fully overgrown by jungle.

Next, we were in Tegucigalpa, capital of Honduras, and visited a different AID-financed effort. In this case, a Honduran private voluntary organization had contracted with AID to establish a cooperative lending bank for small entrepreneurs. One borrower was making soccer and work shoes and needed a loan to buy component materials and pay workers. Another used a loan to buy a commercial oven and display cases in order to start a bakery. In both cases, the borrower had paid back an initial loan and then had borrowed more to expand. Though I believe this cooperative bank was financed with AID cash, in other cases and other countries, food aid has been sold (monetized) to provide such a bank's capital.

Life in the DC Suburb

The DC area was not the open and familiar midwestern environment to which I was accustomed. As I would meet children on the sidewalk while walking our dachshund, Tena, I would greet them, but they would not respond. I understood; they had been warned, I am sure, to not speak to strangers.

Most of our Vienna neighbors, including an especially friendly Filipino couple next door, were at work during the day. The wife of that couple worked at a travel agency in downtown Washington, and her husband worked elsewhere in the city. Their eight-year-old son would come home from school each day to an empty house, so he would often come over to tell me what had happened in school. One afternoon he came directly to our door; he just had to tell someone he had been elected class president! I was glad I was home to hear, and we shared his joy over some freshly baked cookies.

More New Experiences

After I had finished my Volunteer Office work early one afternoon, instead of taking the westbound Orange Line car toward Vienna, I took an eastbound car to Metro Center, transferred to the Red Line, and rode to the Maryland suburbs, the end of the line, just to see the territory. I got off, walked through a suburban shopping mall, and then went back to the station.

I could take the Red Line to Union Station, which was two blocks north of the Senate office buildings, and the Orange Line could take me to Capital South, which was a short walk to either the Capitol Hill Club or the House office buildings. There I might meet Duane for a reception, perhaps for a visiting Kansas or Iowa delegation or, in the case of the Capitol Hill Club, a Republican Party event.

We were also in close proximity to interesting places and beautiful rural countryside of the adjacent states, Maryland and Virginia. We could take weekend drives into Pennsylvania or West Virginia. We saw the miniature horses on Chincoteague Island off the east coast of Maryland and took a ferry to Tangier Island in Chesapeake Bay with former Ames neighbors Gene and Icle Schertz to eat crab cakes.

We were also privileged to host my nephew Dennis Jones and his family,

Cindy, Mindy, and Kristy, for a Fourth of July weekend. We attended an evening concert on the Washington Monument grounds and a morning ceremony at the Jefferson Memorial.

Walking Soybeans

We could also escape the DC area for a three-day weekend at our Iowa farm home. We had a direct flight to Kansas City, and from there it was but a three-hour drive to our farm.

In August I chose to stay at the farm a couple of weeks to prepare to host my relatives coming from Germany. Duane returned to DC; my relatives would in time arrive there, and Duane would accompany them to Iowa. I wanted to impress our visitors with a clean and neat house, a freshly mowed lawn, and our farm. What bothered me most was an adjacent soybean field, where a few weeds had grown taller than the beans. (This was well before genetic resistance in beans allowed for effective herbicides; famers would "walk the beans" to either pull the weeds or cut them off with a curved knife on the end of a long handle.)

I spent a full morning walking the beans. It was a morning with heavy dew, and when I got back to the house at lunchtime, my jeans and boots were soaked. My jeans were clinging so tightly to my legs they would not come off. I tried and tried! For a time, I thought my only options were to sit in the sun for the afternoon, cut my jean legs with scissors, or walk to our neighbors and ask for help!

Mount Washington

In late September 1988, my sister Norma Jean came to visit, and while Duane was at a food aid conference on the Harvard campus in Boston, she and I drove up through eastern Pennsylvania, New York, Connecticut, and Massachusetts to New Hampshire's White Mountains and Mount Washington. Halfway up Mount Washington, glancing from time to time over the edge of the narrow roadway as I drove, I wished we had just viewed the mountain from the valley below. And the drive down was even more thrilling.

We picked Duane up in Boston on Saturday and reached our home in Vienna late that evening.

Family Heritage

DC was within easy driving distance to Virginia's Shenandoah Valley, the base of my maternal grandmother's family, the Kites. We drove to what I believed to be the area from which the Iowa Kites had come, south of Luray. We checked phone books and asked questions. In short order, we were alerted to the Kite Store, alongside Route 340 near Alma. The current owner had recently purchased the store from the Kites, but the Kites still lived in an attractive ranch-style house next door.

From the latter, we were directed to their nearby son, a banker, who had devoted some time to family genealogy. Yes, his records included names of a branch that had migrated to Iowa in the late 1800s. We shared with him nephew Dennis Jones's genealogy interest and would, in turn, relay his contact information to Dennis.

With my sister Norma Jean in a later visit to the Kite
ancestral area near Alma, Virginia.

Other weekends we visited Duane's distant cousin George Acker, who lived on the farm northeast of Martinsburg, Pennsylvania, that their great-great-grandparents had purchased in 1823. It was from that location, in the late 1870s or early 1880s, that five siblings (and their spouses and offspring) of Duane's great-grandparents' generation had headed west. His great-grandparents had settled in Cass County, Iowa; two families had traveled on to Nebraska; and two had headed to northwest Iowa. It appears that, according to the strong German tradition, the eldest son had inherited the farm. George and the other Pennsylvania Ackers we were to meet were his descendants. We yet retain connections to several of the Pennsylvania Acker family.

Beyond the fascination of linking to distant relatives, we found enjoyment and value in driving out into the country after a week or more of the hassle of city life, noise, and traffic. To see and feel the open space, to drive country roads, or to have a picnic lunch on the lawn of a country church or a town park felt good.

Back to Manhattan

After two and a half years in DC, in late December 1988, we moved back to Manhattan so that Duane could return to his first love, teaching the introductory course in animal science. We had purchased a three-bedroom brick ranch home (by video and phone) on Hunting Drive, west of the campus. I would have fun renovating and redecorating.

First, we had a fence built to the east and south of the house for Tena, our dachshund. In the process, we eliminated an existing sidewalk from the front door to the street, in part because it had steps at the far end, and replaced it with a curved walk that ended at street level. A branch from that sidewalk served our back door via the fenced-in backyard.

Inside the house, we opened the wall between two small front bedrooms and installed french doors. The near room would be Duane's study and the far room a guest bedroom. With the french doors open, the space was more open and inviting. To provide a more spacious feel to the dining/living room, we covered the solid east wall—the far wall as one entered the room—with mirrors.

Between the kitchen and front door was a small wood-paneled family room. Again to make it appear more spacious, I filled all the panel crevices with wood filler and painted it off-white. It was a big job, but it made the room, with its fireplace and a TV, more inviting and comfortable.

We also converted two large basement rooms into a student or guest apartment, including a bedroom, bath, and living room. The apartment could be entered from the bottom of our basement stairs or via the basement garage. There was enough open space at the bottom of the stairs and apartment entry that I designed a small lighted pool and waterfall for it, with the water cascading down over stones and the pool lined with plants.

When all was finished, in late spring, we held an open house for many longtime Manhattan friends. I also hosted a shower for the future wife of Kevin Shull, son of our 1960s neighbors on Oregon Lane.

Duane had been asked to continue with AID on a quarter-time basis, especially for his liaison work with Congress and US industry groups. He had an academic year appointment at K-State, teaching both the freshman animal science course and a senior-level course in international agriculture. He would be in Washington a few days each month, and we would be at our Iowa farm for the summer. (Little did we know that after a year we would be drawn back to DC.)

Basketball season was well underway when we arrived back in Manhattan, and we could walk from our house on Hunting Drive to the new Bramlage Coliseum. Fund-raising for that arena had taken place during Duane's presidency. It had been the first multimillion-dollar fund-raising project ever for K-State and had been achieved after years of planning, meeting with and hosting donors, working with architects, and gaining regent approval.

To India

Duane's AID role took him and a couple of team members to Indonesia and Singapore after Christmas that year and then to New Delhi, India, for an international cooperative conference. I had never been to India, so another team member's spouse and I arranged by phone to meet them there. The two of us had never met but got acquainted as we settled in adjoining seats for a transatlantic flight from Dulles Airport.

After two days in Delhi, riding in three-wheel pedal taxis on crowded streets and watching cattle in the parking lot from our hotel window, and a day bus trip to the Taj Mahal, the four of us flew to the state Gujarat on the west edge of India to visit a small village near the city of Anand. There was a free movie in the town park that evening, but our focus was on what was happening at a milk receiving station before the movie began.

Men and women stood in line to deliver their day's milk production from their cow or water buffalo. Most carried a covered metal pail; others had metal or crockery containers balanced on their heads. At the milk receiving window, their container was emptied into a weighing vessel, and they moved on toward a short line at a second window. In the meantime, a small milk sample was taken from the weighing vessel, and an instrument was used to measure, by electrophoresis, the percent fat and nonfat solids in the milk. In less than two minutes, the value of each person's milk was calculated, and each received at the second window a slip of paper showing their milk's weight and composition and their payment in coins or paper money. Then they went to the movie.

This was one of hundreds of such milk receiving stations, all part of a dairy cooperative that had gained international acclaim for enhancing India's milk production and consumption, as well as providing more income for small farmers.

To DC Again

Near the end of 1989, Duane was invited back to Washington. Yeutter, mentioned earlier and recently named secretary of agriculture by President George H. W. Bush, asked Duane to head up a USDA agency that was in difficulty. We sold the house and moved rather quickly, in January 1990, to a two-bedroom apartment on the sixth floor of an eleven-story structure in Crystal City, just across the George Washington Parkway from and overlooking Reagan Airport. From the condo's small balcony we had a good view of the Washington Monument and the fabulous July 4 fireworks over the Potomac.

*Our high-rise in Crystal City, the side that faced the George Washington
Parkway and Ronald Reagan Airport. Our unit was on the sixth floor to
the right of center. Though there was much rail traffic, especially to and from
more-distant suburbs during rush hour, we were oblivious to the sound.*

Returning to the DC area also meant that I could return to the White
House Volunteer Office. Bush had replaced Reagan, so most of the key people
in that office had continued. I enjoyed being back with the group, addressing
cards (in my case penning copperplate), answering the phone, being part of
the welcoming crowd for visiting dignitaries, and helping with the Easter egg
hunt. There were 150,000 Christmas cards to address that year, and Mrs.
Bush had asked William Gimmel to paint the scene for that year's card. Of
course, each of us volunteers received one for our scrapbooks. Again, because
of the volume of cards and my pleasure in doing copperplate, I took envelopes
and lists back to our apartment.

Duane's job as administrator of the Office of International Cooperation
and Development (OICD) and soon the Foreign Agricultural Service (FAS)
as well meant that we were often invited to events at foreign country embassies.
These were always festive occasions, with music, generous food and drink, and
well-decorated halls or lawns.

Following Queen Elizabeth's visit that spring to the White House, Duane
and I were among guests at the British embassy. The grounds were in full
blossom with hanging baskets of colorful flowers. I was again at the front,
standing against the rope as Queen Elizabeth emerged from the embassy to
walk along, wave, and shake a few hands. I was surprised she was not much

taller than me. Apparently she recognized a party behind me, and she reached over my shoulder to shake a hand. One is never too old to not be thrilled at having been touched by the queen!

Apartment Living

Life on the sixth floor of our rather new high-rise was far different from that in the Vienna home we had left a year earlier. There was no lawn or flower garden to tend, and by that time, we were without a dog to walk. I wanted to get acquainted with our building neighbors, so I asked the building manager if there was not a place for a morning coffee gathering for some of the residents. I soon had a response—"Yes, you can use a room on the ground floor"—and management even furnished the coffee, tables, and chairs. In a short time we had a group of about ten people, mostly women and one man whose wife was in the military, and we gathered every Tuesday morning.

A second high-rise was soon built to the north. I knew some of the women who would reside in that building and invited them to join our group, and we adopted the name the Keva Club. The group was a godsend for each of us, a base for developing friendships and arranging activities. We organized some dancing lessons for residents and went as a group for a Saturday-morning DC foreign embassy tour, our group having been asked to help with that event. Duane and I were assigned to the door of one of the embassies to greet visitors and hand out brochures.

When some of the group learned I was doing copperplate calligraphy in the Volunteer Office, they asked me to teach copperplate. In the end, nearly twenty-five people participated, often in small groups, to learn the skill and to practice. I cherish a pillow that the group gave me, their twenty-five signatures embossed on the pillow.

Our Keva group volunteered to serve dinner at an inner-city church on a regular basis, perhaps every two weeks, to street men, some of whom had been hospitalized. The church area was not considered safe for women, so we were glad to have a man as part of our group. We prepared and took a hot meal, likely lasagna. The church hosts provided tablecloths and china plates; our hot food and the setting created a special experience for these men. On one occasion, I noticed a man with a bandage on his wrist and asked if he had broken it. He replied, "Knife cut." I was so innocent!

When I began this writing, more than twenty-five years after leaving DC, I wondered whether the club still existed, with so many changes in administration and Congress and so many building residents associated with the government. A friend recently sent me a Crystal City newsletter, and yes, it does! That gives me even more satisfaction; it had been a godsend for us and is yet one for new residents.

Duane and I had become good friends with one of his fellow administrators and wife, an Illinois couple, Virgil and Thelma Rosendale, he administrator of USDA's Packer and Stockyards Administration. Thelma and I decided we would host a pre-Christmas party in our building for the staff of Duane's and Virgil's agencies and a few other key USDA people with whom they worked. As we had experienced with Duane's AID staff, the turnout was great, and we received a good many thank-you comments.

Time in the Country

Condo life, within a couple of miles of USDA and the White House Volunteer Office and with a Metro station and below ground supermarket and shops just across street, was an easy life. However, living within the confines of tall buildings and masses of people, we felt an even greater need for some time in the country. Unless there was a weekend commitment in DC, such as the embassy tour, we would likely lock the condo midmorning Saturday and head to the Virginia countryside, Maryland's eastern shore, or Pennsylvania; we might even find a bed-and-breakfast for Saturday night.

We also traveled with friends. With former Iowa Staters Jean and Lark Carter, we spent a day at Longwood Gardens in southeastern Pennsylvania. With the Rosendales, we picked peaches on a Virginia mountainside and attended an antique car show in Hershey, Pennsylvania. And former SDSU colleague, Duane Everett, rode with us on a Sunday through some of West Virginia's mountain country.

As we had during our earlier DC tour, we would often take a direct flight to Kansas City on Thursday evening and drive to the farm for the weekend, returning Sunday evening. Federal employment policy called "flex time" allowed bunching work hours so Duane could easily plan three-day weekends.

Agriculture Women to Spain and Morocco

USDA Secretary Ed Madigan (Yeutter had been asked by President Bush to chair the Republican National Committee) had asked Duane to become assistant secretary and, in time, asked if I would be willing to lead a US agriculture women's two-week foreign tour in September. Apparently this was an annual department activity, and that year's tour would be to Spain and Morocco, including the World's Fair, Expo '92. The schedule had been established, and a staff member had been assigned to help with details. My role would be to help select the twenty participants, to be the official spokesperson as we traveled, and to represent the secretary in meetings with ministers of agriculture and other officials in host countries. Of course, USDA's Foreign Agricultural Service attachés in those countries would help with in-country activities.

After a bullfight and then briefing meetings with the ministry of agriculture and Spain's major farm organizations in Madrid, we went to a grain, dairy, and fruit farm near Madrid. Next we traveled southwest by air and bus to farms raising sheep, cattle, and pigs and producing rice, corn, tomatoes, cotton, and sunflowers. We then had a full day at Expo '92 in Seville.

From Seville we crossed the Mediterranean on a ferry to Tangier, Morocco. Four days in that country included a visit to the National Polo Club near Rabat, an opportunity for horseback riding in the countryside (I declined the ride), a trip to the Moroccan king's Arabian horse farm, and then travels on south to see vegetable and seed production, a family-owned feedlot, olive and citrus production, and, of course, the world-known open-air market at Marrakech.

Representing USDA Secretary Madigan in a meeting with Morocco's Ministry of Agriculture leadership.

It was a great experience. I enjoy travel and was honored to represent US agriculture and the secretary.

National Arboretum

Yeutter's wife, Jean, had invited me to serve on the board of the National Arboretum, a several-hundred-acre tract with hundreds of plant species, from roses to bonsai to deciduous trees, located in the northeast section of DC. The arboretum, a unit of USDA, is open to the public and is an attractive and peaceful place to spend a Saturday or Sunday. Duane and I had been to several events at the arboretum, including a testimonial dinner for long-term House committee chairman Jamie Whitten and an Agricultural Research Service dinner recognizing outstanding USDA scientists.

* * * * *

Bush lost his reelection bid in November 1992, and our time in DC would end. We departed Washington on January 20, 1993, for our farm, and it was not practical for me to continue on the arboretum board.

I would need to find some activity to replace the excitement and satisfactions of the White House Volunteer Office.

CHAPTER 6

Back to Open Country

As we prepared to leave the Washington area, Duane asked me where I would like to build a new house. Though we had lived in fourteen different homes in our forty-one years of marriage, only once, when we had purchased a split-level house under construction in Manhattan in 1962, had we had any say in our house's features. Even then, the floor plan had been locked in, the framing complete, and the drywall being applied when we signed the contract. Most of our married life we had lived in university housing—eighteen months in a Pammel Court Quonset at Iowa State, eight years in the dean's house on the SDSU campus, and eleven in the K-State president's home. We had owned five houses, one in each of Stillwater, Ames, and Lincoln and two in Manhattan, all built by others.

Duane said I should have one chance in my life to design a home and have at least some say in where it would be. Every location had been a consequence of his job. He mentioned Atlantic, Des Moines, or perhaps one of the college towns where we had lived. I said, "We ought to build it at the farm; that is where you will be most of the time." He liked my answer.

After Bush's defeat, we spent several weekends visiting open houses in new DC housing developments, gathering ideas on house designs and floor plans that might work in a rural setting. On January 24, 1993, the day after Bush's presidency ended and Bill Clinton was inaugurated, we headed west from DC to our Iowa farm.

We could live in the existing farmhouse, what had been our weekend and vacation retreat for the previous fifteen years, while we chose a site, developed plans, and supervised and helped in construction.

After Duane's father's death fifteen years earlier and our purchase of his sister's interest in the farm, we had made some improvements in the farmhouse. Built in sections, from before 1880 to the early 1900s, it had five bedrooms, four up and one down, living room, dining room, large kitchen, sunroom, and window-enclosed porch, plus a bathroom with tub just off the kitchen. There was a shower in the basement, and the ground floor was air-conditioned. We had added a combination bath and laundry plus a two-car garage beyond the kitchen, built a brick-faced fireplace in what would become a family room (former dining room), and insulated the ground floor, including the space between the ceiling and the second-floor bedrooms. The second floor had largely been used for storage, as the ground floor had been plenty of space for our weekend and vacation use.

After several years' use, we had also finished the second floor. With the help of Duane's cousin Leland Acker and local Camblin Plumbing and Heating, we had built closets in two bedrooms, converted what had been a water-tank room above the kitchen into a third bathroom, replaced some of the plaster with sheetrock, and installed a separate heating and air-conditioning system for that floor.

Of course, I had done much of the painting, and I recall spending several days on an intricate border around the sloping walls of the larger bedroom.

In the intervening years, most of the farm buildings—barns, granaries, silos, henhouse, and machine shed—had become outmoded or simply worn out and had been removed. Only the farmhouse and what we referred to as the horse barn remained. We would tear down that barn; its footprint would be part of our new home's front lawn. Our new home would be built just behind two large trees, a maple and a Siberian elm, each having been volunteer saplings in a wooden windbreak fence between a livestock tank house and an old cattle barn fifty years earlier. The old house, with all the improvements we had made, would be rented; it would be good to have neighbors next door.

We were fortunate to engage a respected local builder, Eddie Jensen, who, in his earlier carpentering years, had worked alongside my father. We outlined some of the features we wanted. Eddie would sketch plans, we would revise, and he would sketch again. By early May the basement had been dug, forms erected for the basement walls, and cement poured, and Eddie had completed the framing and plywood subflooring for the first floor. Then the rains began.

Our new home at the farm, into which we moved in February, 1994. At this writing, we have lived in this house for twenty-five years, more than twice as long as in any other home during our sixty-seven years of marriage.

Farmers want spring rain to help germinate the corn and bean seeds. But not every night. Fortunately, Eddie had chosen treated, water-resistant plywood for the subflooring. It seemed that every morning for at least two weeks, our first task each morning was to squeegee off the overnight rain accumulation so Eddie and his helper could keep on working.

In the meantime, Duane had learned to handle his new Case IH tractor, had attended a few farm auctions to purchase used equipment, and had purchased corn and soybean seed for 114 acres not committed to others for the year. Steve Olsen, who had been renting part of our land, would custom operate that 114 acres and would be joining us the following year in operating our total acreage.

One of Duane's goals, among those we had set our first year in the K-State presidency for things we wanted to do after the presidency, had been to operate his home farm at least a few years. With nearly five decades of technology and crop and animal genetic change from that of his youth, it would be a challenge, a far different business.

During our first tour at Kansas State in 1963, we had purchased some nearby land. In 1968, while at SDSU, we had purchased a farm adjacent to Duane's home 130-acre farm and had later acquired other contiguous tracts. The acreage we had gathered should make for an economic unit.

During corn harvest in the fall of 1996.

I was at the developing new house every day and nearly all day. There were questions to answer, decisions to be made, and details to check. Beyond that, when construction had progressed in early fall to the point of finished sheetrock, I could help our painters, Roger and Steve Mathias. I have always enjoyed painting. I could also measure for curtains and carpet.

Newcomers in Our Home Community

Though this was our home community and we had spent weekends and vacation time there, we were, in most respects, newcomers. And whereas each of our university moves had planted us into an existing social structure of people with mutual interests—a department, a college, or the total university—in this case there was no such structure. It would be, in many ways, a new experience.

The community club of farm wives to which Duane's aunt Mabel Kimball had belonged invited me to join, and I found membership helpful in getting acquainted with and feeling comfortable in the area. I was encouraged by longtime friends Donnis Helbourg and Lois Coomes to join a Questers group, with monthly evening meetings of women who enjoyed discussing and presenting programs on antique furniture and furnishings. I also joined a monthly book club, Browning Club, that had been first organized in 1899.

We joined the local YMCA, made modest use of its facilities, and looked forward to a new facility—with a pool—for which community leaders were seeking funds. We supported that effort, and as soon as it was completed in the early 2000s, I was in the pool early at least three mornings a week and spent many afternoons helping in the pool area with younger swimmers.

Before our move back to the farm, we had had a phone call from longtime friend Tom Magill. He had invited us to become a part of Atlantic's Presbyterian Church, and we soon joined. Within a few weeks of our arrival and attendance, the church organist, Maxine Lyon, and her husband, Walt, invited us to be a part of their bridge club. We found we had connections with others in that club. Cliff Heyne was a brother to our Kansas State wheat geneticist, Elmer Heyne, and Cliff's wife, Marie, had been Duane's sixth-grade music teacher at Wiota. Mac McCormick, as manager of the local Earl May store, had sold us the forty Austrian pine trees we had planted along the farmstead on a weekend thirteen years earlier.

The Number One Bridge Club

A year or so after we moved to the farm, I was also invited to join "Atlantic's Number One Bridge Club," as the members, with some humor, referred to it. Apparently it had been formed in the early 1900s by twelve women whose husbands were members of the Atlantic Rotary Club. The Rotary Club had met for lunch on Tuesdays, so the wives had decided to meet for lunch on the second Tuesday of each month at a member's home for a hosted lunch and an afternoon of bridge. All would wear hats and gloves, and the hostess would use her finest china, crystal, and silver service. According to some of the current members, the club in earlier years had considered itself rather exclusive; to be considered for membership, one's home had to be south of Sixth Street and west of Chestnut Street.

Those features did not characterize the membership at my joining. Though some of the women's husbands had been Rotary members, only Duane was then a member. Of the eleven others—Louise Hunt, Debbie Hunt Repp, Gert Hunt, Becky Hunt, Leanne Pellett, Jane Kay, Jackie Guttenfelder, Mildred Beatty, Sue Leslie, Karen Molgaard, and Margaret Slepsky—eight of their husbands were also farmers, and the other husbands were retired from town-based occupations. And the only members whose homes were south of Sixth Street and west of Chestnut lived on farms southwest of Atlantic.

Duane and I had enjoyed couples' bridge clubs in Ames, our first time in Manhattan, and our eight years in Brookings, but we had played little from the time we had moved to Lincoln. Our duties at the University of Nebraska and back at Kansas State and Duane's travel during our years in DC had precluded becoming part of a regular monthly group. In time, after Duane "retired" from our farm operation and cut back a bit on his consulting and volunteer travel, we felt the need for such social groups. At a country-club dinner with good friends Ray and Joann Underwood in August 2000, they expressed a parallel interest. Their longtime bridge club had fallen apart, and Ray had retired from his heavy travel schedule as marketing director for Walnut Grove. Together we decided to form two groups, a monthly dinner club and a monthly bridge club, with six couples each. For each, the Underwoods would choose and invite two couples; we would do the same.

At this writing, eighteen years later in October 2018, the dinner club is still going strong, but with only three of the original twelve members. The bridge club gave up four months ago, having replaced a number of members over the years and eventually scaling down to four couples, several with health limitations.

With LuAnn living nearby and Diane in Overland Park, Kansas,
and our less hectic schedule than in earlier years, we could enjoy
more times together. Diane on my right, LuAnn on my left.

I would also have more opportunities for time with my sisters. Marilyn on my left, Norma Jean in front.

Political Interests

My work in the White House Volunteer Office, our six-year proximity to federal agency operations, and reading daily both the *Washington Post* and *Washington Times* had fixed in us continued interest in political issues. Consequently, we made ourselves available to Republican candidates and officeholders where we might be of help.

When we arrived back in Iowa, Governor Terry Branstad was readying his campaign for a third four-year term. We attended his next fund-raising event and volunteered to help with the campaign. Also, several of Duane's former Iowa State students, as well as other friends, were either in the state legislature or a local office or would become a candidate for office. It was logical that we become involved.

Over time, we would host in our farm home or shop and machine shed, or cohost at other locations, fund-raisers for Branstad; Senators Charles Grassley and Joni Ernst; Congressmen Greg Ganske, Steve King, and David Young; Branstad's successor, Kim Reynolds; and state cabinet and legislature candidates. As important, perhaps more important, were issues of the local community, county officers, and the five members of our county Board of Supervisors; they warrant the support we can provide. We appreciate these good people's willingness to devote a part of their lives to important issues and to endure the pressures that public service bring.

With Iowa governor Terry Branstad early in his third term.

Branstad gave me an interesting experience, an appointment to the judicial nominating committee for the western Iowa judicial district. Our task was to receive applications from those who sought the district judge positions, interview each, and recommend three candidates for each opening for the governor's consideration. I believe there were seven that first year who called for an interview appointment. Six came to our home, but for the seventh our schedules did not mesh. I interviewed that candidate by phone from Corpus Christi, where Duane and I were attending an agricultural roundtable meeting. This experience exposed me to judicial issues and processes with which I was little acquainted.

Branstad also appointed me to the Iowa Arts Council.

Wesley Retirement Facilities

My most enduring and consequential satisfactions involved selection of the site for a major retirement complex in the Des Moines area. I had been asked to serve on the board of WesleyLife, which then owned and operated retirement complexes in five Iowa communities, including Atlantic. We met quarterly, usually at the administrative office in Des Moines and sometimes at one of the complexes.

Duane and I had become close to the Atlantic facility, Heritage House. His parents and all his Acker uncles had contributed modest funds when it had been constructed in the 1960s, and his father had been living in it at the time of his death.

Atlantic's facility was forty years old and needed attention, and perhaps I could help the two other foundation board members from the Atlantic area, Nick Hunt and Dr. Keith Swanson, bring that about. I don't know whether my presence was a factor, but it was during my two three-year terms on the board that a major addition to the Atlantic facility—three one-story "pods," one for Alzheimer patients—was decided upon, planned, and constructed. I enjoyed being involved in some of the plan details, working with the architect and staff, and watching construction.

Then came the board meeting in which the location of a new facility for the Des Moines metropolitan area would be determined. A benefactor had provided several million dollars, and there was not space near Wesley Grand, the foundation's premier complex on Des Moines's West Grand Avenue. In earlier board discussions it had seemed that a downtown location was presumed, at least by several board members. That bothered me; it did not seem logical.

Most of Des Moines's growth was in the western suburbs. Two of the area's major hospitals had established new facilities there, and new homes, apartment and condo complexes, and a vast shopping center had covered many square miles. Further, a facility of the capacity envisioned needed acres of space. It should have a central multistory structure for both residents and health care, open land for duplexes or condos, and perhaps even walking paths among trees and flowers. That was the obvious trend and obvious need. Could that space be found in the downtown area? And if found by clearing existing structures, at what cost?

It was apparent other women on the board were also bothered by the presumption. Action on the location was likely for the afternoon session, so we women had a caucus over lunch.

Soon after the board reconvened, the location issue was pushed for a vote. We women individually made the case for open land in the western Des Moines expansion area. A bit to our surprise, considering the earlier presumed location, the open land got the votes!

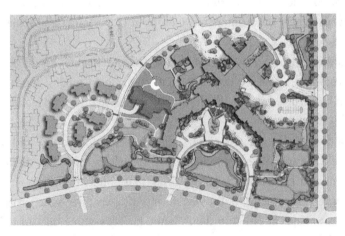

A current plat of Edgewater, WesleyLife's retirement complex on the west edge of Des Moines. Note the lakes and walks, as well as space for future retirees' homes, all important features. (Reprinted with permission of the Ministries of WesleyLife.)

Several years later, as we considered adding a swim spa to our farm home (for my love of swimming), we felt it wise to check out options for our own future before making the investment. Should we plan to remain in our farm home for the duration or eventually accommodate ourselves in Atlantic's Heritage House, in Florida, or in Edgewater, the new facility in Des Moines's western suburb? We visited Edgewater. We were impressed by the facility's pool and spa, the openness of its apartments, its café, and the open land where several duplexes were being built and residents were enjoying a walk. I felt that day an intense quiver of satisfaction.

Though impressed by Edgewater, we demurred. We added the room and spa to our farm home.

CHAPTER 7

I Pick Up My Brushes

After we settled in our new home, I needed more things to do or in which to be involved. Though I enjoyed the groups I had become a part of, my new friends, and the political activity, life on the farm, seven miles from a town of seven thousand people, was yet quite a change from my rewarding work in the White House Volunteer Office.

I noticed in the local newspaper that a china-painting club in Walnut, Iowa, about twenty miles from our farm, was holding a show. That caught my attention; painting had given my mother much satisfaction.

My interest in art goes back to my school days at Washington No. 4, art lessons in the monthly teachers' magazines that my teacher had shared. During my high school years I had saved money and purchased an art correspondence course. Early in our marriage, when our daughters were but toddlers, I had done several paint-by-numbers scenes. And, doing water colors in the Kansas Flint Hills had given me more confidence.

I went to the Walnut show, learned there was a local porcelain-painting club, Nishna Valley China Dolls, and I joined. Though I had done considerable work with watercolors while at Kansas State, porcelain painting was much more complex, and I had much to learn. Helen Blunk, who had once lived on a neighboring farm, helped me with the basics, and she and other club members showed me their work.

However, monthly meetings were not enough for me. Soon club members Mildred Weir, Dolores Hansen, Blunk, and sometimes Mildred Auerbauch were coming to our home an afternoon each week to paint and comment on each other's work. They all gave me encouragement.

I then needed an electric firing kiln to fix each layer of applied paint, and our attached garage was the logical place. What we painted one week would be fired and ready for the next paint layer the following week. Painting on porcelain quickly became my major focus, occupying every afternoon, and I was doing so many pieces I needed a second kiln.

Porcelain painting captured my interest because it is the most challenging. In addition to perspective, color, and shading, porcelain demands attention to effects of firing temperature and duration on individual pigments and their oil carrier. After each layer of paint is applied, starting with the lighter shades, the piece is fired, and the firing temperature may range from 1,400 degrees Fahrenheit to as high as 2,300 degrees. Only with experimentation, supplemented by the advice and experience of others, can one establish the combination that will yield the tone and brilliance of color one seeks. My painting desk holds dozens of work materials, tubes of pigment powder, and bottles of oils.

Mention of porcelain or china painting usually triggers thought of flowers on dinnerware. With other club members, I also painted flower designs on vases, cups, pitchers, boxes, and other small items. I gained experience mixing pigments with oils and with firing. In due time, I tried my hand at geometric and other designs on plates. Next I considered porcelain tile, wall or floor tile, and that opened a rewarding option: finished pieces could be framed and put on the wall. I began to paint landscapes and scenes that featured birds and animals. These all gave me more challenges and, therefore, more satisfaction.

*With one of my early and larger pieces. Blue is my favorite
color, especially when it is a state fair ribbon!*

Though China's porcelain is well known by global travelers, with the country's porcelain featured in its cultural museums and historic displays, there is also a rich porcelain history in Western Europe, especially Germany. These countries have the quality clays needed for the finest porcelain stock, and the countries' nobility of early centuries had the resources to train and develop artists to a high level of skill.

While in Germany with friends in the early 2000s, Duane and I took a train side trip to the city of Dresden and its Meissen china factory, considered the zenith of porcelain. We watched the Meissen artists at work and marveled at their skill and productivity. Our factory hosts told us that during WWII German citizens as well as the factory artists had hid their porcelain treasures underground, in mines and caves, so they would be safe from the repeated and intense Allied bombings. Some, unfortunately, had been taken by either German or occupying forces, but in 1956 about 750 pieces had been returned to Dresden.

After Duane retired from his farming operation and was doing more traveling, I took over his farm "office" adjacent to our kitchen and overlooking our fields. His former bookcase and a cabinet gave me room for my pigments and oils, and his desk was perfect for my work space and files. I would do my house and garden work in the morning, and every afternoon, with the TV turned on low to follow political news, I would be at work. With the garage kiln just a few steps away, I could be rather productive, applying a paint layer to one or more items while others were being fired. We soon had a display shelf installed above the windows of our dining/family room as well as a series of display shelves in my painting "office."

Shows and Winnings

The local painting club sponsored several shows, at Heritage House, at a church, or in an otherwise vacant Main Street store during a town festival. Encouraged by Blunk and other club members, I entered some of my work at a regional show, and several pieces earned ribbons.

Next for me was the Iowa State Fair. For five years I entered three to five pieces each year, and each year my pieces would receive some ribbons—red or white (second or third place in a class) and sometimes blue, meaning I had won the class. Several years Blunk and I also spent one or more days at the fair demonstrating our techniques to fair visitors.

By the end of my fifth year of showing, I had received five blues, and I decided, *Five blues in five years is enough. I should retire from state fair competition and just have fun painting.*

At the Iowa State Fair, two of my blue-ribbon pieces on the top shelf.

A local arts council had formed in the early 1990s, and with my having shown some items at a local art show, I was invited to become a part of the council. And, in time, Governor Branstad appointed me to the Iowa Arts Council. Meetings of the council in Des Moines plus conventions and state shows of the Iowa Porcelain Painters Association gave me a number of acquaintances across the state.

Now Fiberglass

After experimenting with geometric designs on dinnerware and moving on to landscapes, animals, and birds, I learned one might add texture, such as for animal fur, tree bark, or even fabric, with fiberglass. Perhaps I could blend a bit of fiberglass into a layer of paint and fix both to the porcelain stock in the firing process.

I purchased a few small sheets of fiberglass at a local body shop. My first effort was on a tall vase; the design would include a diagonal ribbon of colored "fabric." For the third or fourth layer of paint on the "fabric," I teased out some fiberglass, worked it into the wet paint, and placed the piece in the kiln. I knew that to fix the fiberglass into the porcelain, the piece had to be fired for a longer time than for the paint. It worked! After several layers of paint and fiberglass and repeated firing, the outcome was great!

My next effort with fiberglass was owls on the branches of a tree. To me, considering artistic license, the fiberglass made the bark of that tree trunk appear almost natural.

Fiberglass fused into the paint gives texture to the "fabric" embellishment on the card box. For the painting of the owls, I used fiberglass to help simulate tree bark. The latter piece is one of which I am most proud, for both the owls and the tree bark.

I had had experience with fiberglass in earlier years, perhaps with a task that will surprise the reader. Though there was a bit of artistry to it, art was not the purpose. It was about 1960, eight years into our marriage, and the front fenders of our 1955 Ford, exposed to years of winter road salt from Iowa streets and highways, were rusted through behind the front wheels. Duane chipped out the rusted and weak metal and stuffed wads of newspaper into the voids. I mixed the fiberglass components and with a putty knife applied layers of the fiberglass mix, to achieve or exceed the lower fender curvature. After the fiberglass had dried solid, Duane sanded it to refine the curvature, and I applied a spray paint that matched.

That experience was also a success. When we sold the Ford on leaving Manhattan in late January 1966, those fenders appeared as solid as when the car was new.

Shirley Hansen Acker

Teaching in Florida

By the early 2000s, we were considering an optional location for Iowa winters. Because of our longtime link to Iowa State, friends in Ames, and proximity to the farm, we sought to rent a small condo for a month, February 2002, at Ames's Green Hills. Finding no rental, we purchased a one-bedroom condo on the eighth floor of Green Hills' high-rise with an open view of the countryside. We found at Green Hills twenty-two people we knew, including former colleagues, fellow students, and even parents of former students, and we renewed our relationships. There was also convenient transportation to basketball games and concerts, and it was a short city bus ride to the campus for seminars. We thoroughly enjoyed the month.

We retained ownership of that unit for a time; it might entice us to spend a few weekends there for ball games or other events. However, by the end of 2002, we had used the condo only once. We also had found that the February wind in Ames was as cold as it had been in the 1950s and '60s.

We spent February 2003 in a rented double-wide in Estero, Florida, and by the end of the month had purchased a first-floor condo in a then new over-fifty-five community, now called Pelican Preserve, a few miles north of the Fort Myers airport. We put the Green Hills condo on the market; Florida would be our choice for the winter. At this writing, January 2019, we are enjoying our sixteenth winter in Pelican Preserve.

Pelican Preserve is the type of community where many residents are seeking to develop new hobbies and skills. I tried my hand early with several hobbies related to the visual arts, and when some of my new friends learned of my interest and experience with porcelain, they asked if I would teach a class. What a challenge that turned out to be!

Twenty-four people wanted to enroll, so I scheduled two groups, with each meeting for three hours twice a week. As any teacher of skills would know, my commitment was not only the time in class but also the time to gather their work materials, in this case pigments and oils. I also had to see that the kiln, also used by a ceramics group, was cleaned and free of any clay fragments or dust before we placed freshly painted pieces in for firing. I enjoyed teaching, but with cleaning the kiln and firing my students' pieces, it was a seven-day-a-week task, with some days extending into evening.

Several members of my beginners' class at Pelican Preserve show their work.

I taught those classes for two years, and a few asked that I teach an advanced class. It had been fun, and I had had many satisfactions, but I decided to retire from the teaching profession. I encouraged those who had been captured by porcelain painting to simply paint for their own pleasure and satisfaction. We purchased a kiln for our condo, and I would do the same.

It's difficult to estimate the number of pieces I have done. Shelves, a plate rail, and our walls hold many. Many others have been given away, several to local fund-raising auctions or events but most to friends near and far.

Though I might have been disappointed in the final appearance of some—reds, especially, lose their luster or brightness during firing—every piece has given me satisfactions. I am especially proud of several pieces, with animals, birds, or original designs or where I fused fiberglass to achieve texture. Photos of most of my pieces are stored on a series of CDs, many of the photos by friend Kerry Barrett, and several were selected for a coffee-table book Duane and I put together.

Copies of this coffee-table book of some of my pieces are held in the South Dakota State University and Kansas State University art center libraries.

* * * * *

From where did I come to these many unexpected and rewarding experiences? What in my ancestry or my early years foretold what I would seek to do or how I would function? Why did I so enjoy hosting university faculty, students, and others? From where did my interest in art come? Why do I so enjoy swimming and walking? Why am I so cautious with money, so fiscally conservative? Why was I so thrilled to see the wild animals on Kenya's Serengeti? Why am I always seeking a new challenge or ready for a new experience? Maybe my first twenty years, as detailed in the next chapter, will give the reader—or me—some clues.

CHAPTER 8

Little Vitcup

Dr. Agnes Wilder's houseman drove her the seven miles west of Atlantic to our farm and its two-story frame house to help Mother with my birth. It would reach five degrees below zero that night, January 29, 1932. Wilder lived at the southeast corner of Eighth and Chestnut, had her office in her home and a cage full of monkeys on her back porch. In the years to come, I would look forward to my checkups; I could watch her monkeys through her living/waiting room window.

Records tell me I weighed eight pounds and was nineteen inches long. I was the second daughter born to my parents, Lula and Henry Otto Hansen, three years after my older sister, Norma Jean. Eight years later there would be another sister, Marilyn.

Yet innocent and sweet at three years.

113

A Bit of Ancestry

My only living grandparents at the time of my birth were my father's parents, Christina and Carsten Hansen. Each had come from Germany to the U.S. as children with their parents, likely in the 1870s, their families settling in the Walnut, Iowa, area. They married and farmed northeast of town. By the time I came along, they had retired and lived in a white stucco house on the northeast edge of Walnut. One of my early memories is Grandpa sitting in his lounge chair, smoking a cigar.

Mother's maiden name was Longnecker, and her parents had come to the Walnut area from near the Winnebago Indian encampment north of Omaha, Nebraska. They later divorced, and my grandmother died of cancer while my mother was yet in her youth, so my mother then lived with her older sister, Ada, and Ada's husband, Julius Mueller, on their farm, also northeast of Walnut.

I have no knowledge of Grandfather Longnecker's ancestry, but my maternal grandmother was a Kite, and that family had migrated to Iowa from Virginia.

From my parents' marriage in 1921, they had lived on and operated as tenants the 160-acre Mueller farm, where Mother had spent her more recent years. The Muellers lived in the farm's major house; Dad and Mother lived in an adjacent, older tenant house.

History from Dad's Ledger

Dad's ledger, a worn, taped, and re-taped five-by-thirteen-inch order book that he maintained from 1921 through 1953, tells us he farmed the cropland on a 60:40 crop-share basis, he providing the machinery and labor and receiving 60 percent of the corn or oats produced. He paid Mueller eighty dollars cash rent the first year for ten acres of pasture, forty-three acres of hay ground, and the three acres their house and yard occupied. The ledger also discloses that fifty acres of oats yielded 1,950 bushels (thirty-five per acre), of which Dad's share was 1,170 bushels. The sixty-one acres of corn yielded 3,660 bushels (sixty per acre), and Dad's share was 2,196 bushels.

That ledger was not limited to farm finances; it shows all family expenses and income from October 1921, when Dad was apparently getting ready for that tenancy. The first recorded purchases were fifty dollars for an engine, five dollars for a mower, and ninety dollars for a wagon. In early 1922 he paid fifty dollars for a hay-loader, ten dollars for a hayrack, and sixty dollars for a drill, the latter purchased from Mueller, his landlord and brother-in-law.

Dad had likely saved any money he made working for his father and perhaps neighbors between his school years and the time he married Mother. Later ledger entries, including interest from or sale of war bonds, suggest such savings.

Enough of Tenant Farming

By late 1928, in their seventh year of marriage, Mother and Dad apparently had had enough of being tenant operators and had likely accumulated some savings. Their annual income those seven years, 1922 through 1928, had averaged $3,384, with expenses of $2,122. That October they purchased an eighty-acre farm south of Walnut and west of Atlantic, where I would be born. According to the ledger, they paid $175 per acre for the farm, with $1,000 down payment on October 9 and another $5,000 paid on October 26, when they received the deed.

There is also a January 29, 1932, expense entry: "Dr. Agnes Wilder, Shirley's birth. $35."

Our Farmhouse

Our house had apparently been built not long before my parents' 1928 purchase. It was larger and more modern than most farm homes at the time, especially with its indoor toilet and electricity. I would learn that a few years earlier the farm owners between our farm and Atlantic had organized a cooperative to build the power transmission line, with each buying their electricity from the generating plant in Atlantic.

Our farmstead was on the south side of the road, and our house had an open porch and "front" door on the east, facing the driveway. The front door opened to the parlor on the right and the dining room on the left. A guest bedroom, which served as a coatroom when the Hansen family came for Sunday dinner or neighbors came to play cards, was in the northwest corner.

The kitchen and pantry were to the southwest, the family kitchen table near a west window, with a view to the road. That view was important; Dad could wave at a passing neighbor from the table, often in response to Clarence Peterson's or another's car horn's quick beeps, to the rhythm of "Shave and a haircut, six bits."

There were four bedrooms on the second floor, mine in the northeast corner. The northwest room doubled as playroom and storage and had a large trunk full of dress-up clothes, dolls, and toys.

We also had a full basement with cement floor, where we could roller-skate. Among my best memories is skating with my older sister, Norma Jean, or neighbor kids, who loved to come visit so they could skate. There were small rooms or bins for cobs, wood, and coal, plus space for Mother's wringer washing machine. Monday was always wash day.

Most of our daily traffic was via an enclosed south porch off the kitchen, and I recall an icebox on that porch. There was no heat on the porch, so ice was needed only in the summer. Our first refrigerator was purchased, according to Dad's ledger, in 1943, when I was twelve.

Hauling Coal from Carbon

Corncobs and wood Dad had cut were the major furnace fuel, but coal was needed to keep a fire going through the night.

When we drive today from our Iowa farm to Kansas City, we sometimes go through the small town of Carbon. Carbon was once home to many who worked the mines southwest of town. Today it has fewer than twenty homes, some vacant. The mines shut down decades ago; their high-sulfur-content coal had lost its market.

In the 1930s, however, the mines were active, and Carbon coal was the closest and cheapest. I recall a long ride with Dad to Carbon for coal. It was perhaps early November, and his truck was likely a late Model T Ford. We had taken along sandwiches to eat on the way home.

At the mine we drove onto a scale to weigh the empty truck, then under a big hopper. Handling coal was a dirty job; all the workers' overalls were nearly black. The truck lurched and dropped a few inches as the coal was dumped on. We then drove back across the scale, and Dad paid for the coal.

Back home, midafternoon, Dad scooped the coal down a chute through a north basement window. By the time he was done, his overalls were also black.

From the Farm to Walnut

The mid-1930s was the depth of the Great Depression, especially hard on farmers, and Dad's doctor had told him that he likely had a stomach ulcer and should get away from the stress of farming. He held an auction in December 1935 to dispose of his equipment and livestock, and we moved to Walnut the following February. My world would change.

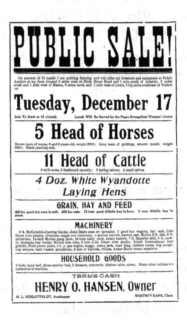

The sale bill for Dad's auction of equipment and livestock. He posted these bills at weekly livestock auctions and other locations. He paid $5.10 for printing the bills and paid the Atlantic News Telegraph $12.80 "for advertising," printing the bill in several editions. He paid the auctioneer, H. L. Schotloffel, $24.05 (1 percent of the sale proceeds, $2,404.50), for "crying the sale."

It was in the dead of winter—February 6, 1936, according to Dad's ledger—that a big grain truck, Jacobsen Bros. scrolled on the cab's door, rolled into our farmstead. A young neighbor, Alfred Brehmer, also arrived, and he helped Dad and the trucker load our furniture. We followed the truck in our family car to where we would live, Aunt Lucy's house, two blocks north and a block east of Walnut's one-block "downtown." Aunt Lucy, then recently deceased, had been a sister of my Hansen grandfather. The ledger tells us Dad paid Brehmer two dollars for his help and Jacobsen Brothers eight dollars for hauling our goods the twelve miles to Walnut.

Dad had rented our farm to the Thurmans, recently married neighbors. Years later, after Dad's death, the Thurmans would tell me they could never thank my father enough for "helping them get their financial life in order." The Thurmans were to pay cash rent, but when December came and the crop had been harvested, they did not have enough money to pay the rent. Dad, then working at a Walnut gasoline station, forgave all or most of the debt. There are no farm-income entries for 1936 and 1937 in Dad's ledger.

By early summer, "Uncle Dave" Kite, an uncle of my mother who was in declining health, invited our family to move two blocks south to live with him. Mother could take care of him in exchange for rent.

Chimney Fire?

As I sat in Uncle Dave's south bay window, I spotted a few sparks floating down, just visible in the gathering dusk. Then it was a flow, a mass of sparks. I yelled for Mother, and soon the Walnut fire truck, red light flashing, had sped the four blocks to the house. A couple of volunteer firemen stood in the side yard looking up at the roof.

In the end, there was no fire. The sparks were just the consequence of the first furnace fire of the fall season. The updraft of the roaring fire had sucked loose and ignited accumulated soot—perhaps even some leaves—inside the chimney.

On Grandpa's Lap

It was during these two years in Walnut that I got to know well my Hansen grandparents. They lived only a block away, and I was often in their house visiting with my grandmother. She was so sweet and kind and usually had freshly baked bread. Grandpa Hansen would sit in his overstuffed chair in the living room. He called me his "little Vitcup"; I assume that meant "little blonde" or "little one" in the colloquial German of his youth. At a family gathering or when I might be spending a day or a week with them, he would lift me, his little Vitcup, onto his lap. It was a comfortable place to be, and I felt privileged.

In those two years I became more acquainted with my then only cousin, Ralph Hansen (I would have only three cousins). He was the son of Dad's brother George and his wife, Ella, and they lived on what had been my grandparents' farm north of Walnut. They later had a daughter, Helen. Dad's sister Willinda and her husband, Andy, owned and lived in a large apartment house in Omaha and later had a son, Roy.

When Aunt Linda and Uncle Andy hosted the Hansen Sunday dinner at their home in Omaha, we would take along Grandma and Grandpa Hansen. Mother, Grandma, Norma Jean, and Marilyn would be packed in the back seat; I, Grandpa's "little Vitcup," would be squeezed between him and Dad in the front.

It was good that the "little Vitcup" nickname was only between Grandpa and me and in my early years. Had it been known to my later schoolmates at Washington No. 4, it might have stuck as my handle through the eighth grade.

School in Walnut

Uncle Dave's house was within a block of the Walnut school, a large red brick structure, where I would start first grade in the fall of 1937. Miss Robinson was my teacher, and I loved school. I also had a special friend, Willa Croft, who lived next door to Grandma and Grandpa Hansen, and we spent a lot of time together. Our friendship may have started even before my family moved to Walnut, when I would stay with my grandparents. Six decades later, after Duane and I moved back to our Iowa farm, I would reestablish and appreciate even more my friendship with Willa, by then widowed and working in an Atlantic shop.

Back to the Farm

Dad's health improved by early 1938, and we moved back to the farm. Though again an independent farm family, farm prices were yet low and farm income meager, so Dad worked away from home many days, for other farmers and doing carpentry and painting.

The ledger shows, in addition to pay from other farmers, that he earned thirty-five dollars for painting schoolhouses Nos. 8 and 9 (presumably Washington Township) in July 1939, and he painted Nos. 3 and 9 in Pymosa Township in August 1940. I recall he also had a painting partner, Henry Stier, who lived on an acreage on the east edge of Atlantic, and together they painted many houses and farm buildings in the Atlantic and Walnut areas.

Dad also earned a few dollars for selling—or at least encouraging the purchase of—tractors and cars for the Osler company of Walnut. Five such entries from 1938 to 1941 range from five dollars to twenty-four dollars. And, for a time, he worked part-time at a gasoline station, the White Rose, at the west edge of Atlantic.

From 1941 through 1944, Dad also worked part-time for the Agricultural Adjustment Administration (AAA), a USDA agency, measuring farmers' fields to determine crop acreage for AAA payments, subsidies for limiting production or for conservation work. His ledger shows periodic payment checks from $7.50 to $22 for that work and one larger check, $224, likely his own farm subsidy.

Washington No. 4

Instead of the one block to the Walnut school, Norma Jean and I would walk nearly two miles to Washington No. 4, a one-room structure a quarter mile west, a mile south, and then west again across Indian Creek from our farm home. It was a little-traveled dirt road, with no houses the entire distance.

For what would be seven-plus years at No. 4, I would have but one classmate, Doris Peterson. There would be a total of eight to ten students in the school, some coming or going as tenant families moved, usually on March 1, into or from the school district. The only continuing students were Doris and Daryl Peterson and Clifford, Norma Jean, and Howard Christensen. The Christensens lived just west of us, and we would usually meet at the corner between our two farms to walk together.

At Washington No. 4 with my only classmate, Doris Peterson (right), and Ivadell Marxen, who was one grade ahead.

When it was raining or snowing, Mr. Christensen would sometimes haul us to school in a horse-drawn wagon. Dad would likely have left home early to paint or do carpentry work, and Mother did not drive. (Years earlier, while driving down a hill, one of her car's front wheels came off. The front of the car dropped to the ground, and she watched the wheel roll on down the hill. She never drove again.)

At Christmastime we students drew names and would purchase a small gift for the name we drew. In these difficult times, little money was spent on frills. I received a small bottle of Jergens lotion my first Christmas in the school and was thrilled. Never before had I had my own lotion!

A favorite recess game was "Andy over," where one group would throw a softball over the school roof to a group on the other side. One morning, the ball hit the roof, then rolled back and wedged behind the chimney. Being the smallest, I was chosen to fetch the ball. Hoisted up by my teammates to the edge of the roof, I crawled up to the chimney and retrieved the ball. I had been willing to do it, but it was likely one of the school happenings that we did not bother to tell Mother about.

My small size would also determine how I was cast in a school play, as Pee Wee Pork Chop. My sister Norma Jean was cast as my older brother, and we carried on what was to be a humorous dialogue. I don't recall the dialogue theme, but it was apparently a hit with the audience. Word got around the township, and we were invited to perform at the neighboring school, Washington No. 3.

After the two Norma Jeans finished the eighth grade, young Howard would often take a shorter route to school, cross the Indian Creek Bridge to the west and walk the fields directly south to the school. So for my last three years, it was usually just me for the nearly two lonesome miles. Mother had often instructed, "Never ride with a stranger!" If I spotted a rare car coming my way, I would jump into the ditch and hide in the weeds or tall grass until it passed. I sometimes took a shortcut through Dad's pasture. If the bull was nearby, I would stick close to the fence.

My first and favorite teacher at No. 4, Irene Miller, subscribed to several teachers' magazines, and when she married and had to resign (rural schoolteachers could not be married), she gave me her entire collection. I especially enjoyed the artwork described, and I clipped out and kept many of the articles. Miss Miller knew I dreamed of being a teacher, and I read the magazines with both pleasure and anticipation.

Several older girls our family knew had qualified to teach in the country schools through a "normal training" program then available to seniors in Atlantic High School, and that became my plan. However, well before my senior year in Atlantic, country schools would be on the way out, and the program would be discontinued.

After Miller, we had several teachers in succession, sometimes two or three in one year and some just out of high school. When I was in the sixth grade, sitting on the corner of the teacher's desk hearing about her weekend date, we heard a car enter the school driveway. "Must be the country superintendent," she said and quickly briefed all of us on "what we have been working on this morning!"

My favorite pastime was reading, especially the Nancy Drew, Judy Bolton, Hardy Boys, and other series books. But first, after our walk home from school, Norma Jean and I would run to the radio and listen to the serial escapades of Jack Armstrong, Captain Midnight, and Little Orphan Annie.

Farm Chores

Both Mom and Dad were hard workers and gave Norma Jean and me farm chores. Every Saturday we would carry bushels of grain from the corncrib granary to the barn for Dad's five or six milk cows, each of us holding one side of the heavy basket. During the summer we were responsible for the lawn.

My parents were fastidious. Pushing the lawn mower was hard enough, but cutting the grass between the fence wires with scissors was both difficult and tedious. Dad's tools were always in place, and if we borrowed one of them, we made sure we put it back in place. And his Allis Chalmers Model C tractor was always wiped clean after use and before the machine shed door was closed.

By both necessity and habit, my parents were also frugal. I find no expenditures in Dad's ledger to Olsen's Atlantic grocery, where, from my early memory, we purchased our groceries. The obvious reason was Dad would take one or two fifteen-dozen cases of eggs in Olsen's back door and trade the eggs for the few groceries the family needed, perhaps flour, sugar, salt, vinegar, or, for our school lunch sandwiches, minced ham. Mother had a large garden, a strawberry bed, grapevines, and apple, cherry, and peach trees. The garden yielded vegetables and fruit for the summer and, with Mother's extra work, canned goods for the winter. Dad or a neighbor would sometimes butcher a hog or calf, the meat split between families.

Fun on the Farm

Alfalfa harvest (making hay) was a more exciting time on the farm because neighbors worked together. We kids would always go along, and the mothers would often help each other with the noon meal. At our farm, Dad would have mowed the hay and, after it had dried a day or two, raked it into windrows. Neighbors would then come to help. The dry hay was loaded onto a rack, and at the barn a large hayfork on the end of a heavy rope was used to grab a portion of the load. The rope was threaded through a pulley above the open haymow door, other pulleys beyond, and attached to a horse. The horse then pulled the loaded hayfork up and through the large hayloft door, and at a signal by the man in the loft, the hay was dropped.

One year, Howard and Norma Jean Christensen came along with their father and older brother, Cliff, who would help Dad with the hay. While the men were in the field loading the dried hay, we would have some fun, pull each other up into the hayloft with the rope. Being the smallest—and willing—I went first. I grabbed hold of the rope, and the other three, up in the loft, would pull me up.

The hayloft door hung down on the outside of the barn, and I had not thought about the sharp nail points sticking out of the door's exposed side. Twenty feet off the ground, I encountered those sharp points. The others struggled as I braced myself away from the door. They finally got me to a point where they could reach me, and they pulled me up and over the door's threshold. I had only a few scrapes on my legs. Likely another item we did not tell Mother about.

For a time we had a dog, a white Spitz that had wandered onto our farm and we adopted. We called him Snowball, and he was a part of our family until dying of old age.

We also had a player piano, a standard upright with a foot-operated winding mechanism that could play a song with the help of an installed paper roll. As the paper was rolled from its spool to an uptake spindle, air blowing through the hundreds of tiny rectangular perforations would strike companion piano keys and, thus, play the tune. The player piano was more fun than piano lessons and a fascinating curiosity to our neighborhood friends.

Yes, I took piano lessons, but not for long. I think I frustrated my teacher; my hands were so small my digits could not span an octave. After only a few lessons, my teacher and I agreed that piano lessons were not a good investment for my parents. However, through the years, I learned to pick out a few tunes and enjoyed playing.

Perhaps the major diversion for the family was a four-couple card group that gathered every Friday night after corn harvest and continued until field work resumed in late March. It included the Christensens, Petersons, and Zellmers and apparently had gotten started with a duck soup supper after Dad or another had shot some ducks. Every Friday night we were in one of the couple's homes. The men played pinochle, we children played games in a back bedroom (or skated in our basement), and our mothers visited. A late lunch ended the evening. Though the weekly party was referred to as "Duck Soup," I believe the actual duck soup was a one-time event.

Uncle Andy and Pinochle

There were also Hansen family dinners, usually to celebrate wedding anniversaries or birthdays, and they were always on a Sunday, after church. No matter the location, after dinner the men would gather at the kitchen table for a game of pinochle. Though Grandpa Hansen may have lost a bit of his eyesight, he seemed to know where every card was and freely commented on any foolish play. Dad and Uncle George were old hands and could hold their own. However, Linda's husband of two decades, Uncle Andy, was clearly the outsider and usually bore the brunt of Grandpa's barbs.

I paid little attention to the pinochle game until Duane and I started dating and he was included in the family dinners. He would be invited to join the game, but he always declined, saying he would just watch. I was not able to tell whether Andy actually knew less about the game or whether he was just a tempting target for Grandpa. Regardless, Andy never backed away and was always at the table.

The Train Derailment

Early morning in the summer of 1939, the radio, our exposure to the wider world, told us a train had derailed on the east edge of Avoca. It had happened during a rain and hail storm as the train was crossing a bridge over the east branch of the West Nishnabotna River. We rushed through breakfast—Dad had milked before breakfast—and jumped into Dad's brand-new two-door Chevrolet. (Dad's ledger tells us that he paid Osler's $500 for the car on July 4. He would buy a heater for the car before winter, $16.44 on September 25.)

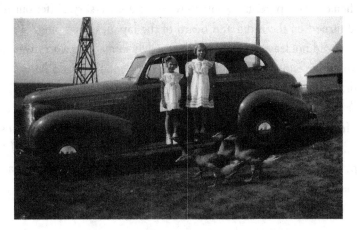

Norma Jean and me beside Dad's 1939 Chevrolet.

The Rock Island tracks from Atlantic to Omaha then ran along the south edges of Marne, Walnut, and Avoca and then, from Minden, followed Mosquito Creek downstream to Council Bluffs. From the top of the hill east of Avoca, we saw the derailment had attracted a big crowd. Autos lined both sides of Highway 83. Cars ahead of us were leaving the highway and entering a field to the left, and Dad followed. We could get closer to the accident site by foot.

At the field gate was a farmer holding out his hat. We then realized we were headed into an oat field, the crop pretty well beaten down. Dad dropped a coin or two into the hat and then related the farmer's comment to the rest of us: "What the chinch bugs hadn't already gotten, last night's hail did. I figured I just as well make the field a parking lot."

We parked and walked up to the site, where a half dozen passenger and freight cars were off the track and in the oats field, some on their side, others tilting. On ahead, one freight car was dangling from the creek bridge. Broken fruit crates, oranges, grapefruit, and apples were scattered on the creek bank, fruit floating in the water.

Until Pearl Harbor two years later, the train derailment was the largest "tragedy" of which I had been aware.

Pearl Harbor

We learned about Pearl Harbor after a Sunday Hansen family gathering at our home for my parents' twentieth wedding anniversary. After our relatives left, we turned on the radio and heard of the Japanese bombing. We were in shock and did not leave the radio for hours. My immediate worry was whether Dad would have to go help fight the war, but I soon realized he was too old to be drafted.

We followed the war news by radio. I watched the sky for P-38 or other planes from the Offutt Air Base near Omaha as I walked to and from school. I even dreamed of being a pilot—what fun it would be! Of course, I had no concept that, at four feet and eleven inches, I could not have seen over a plane's instrument panel.

4-H

Rural youth were invited to become members of 4-H, with separate girls' and boys' clubs in the township. Norma Jean had joined the township club, Washington Workers, and I joined as soon as I reached ten, the minimum age. My first project, for showing at the 1941 Cass County Fair, was a sewing box, made from a cigar box I had painted and decorated.

Perhaps my most memorable 4-H experience was our club's weeklong campout in Atlantic's Sunnyside Park log cabin. Except for weeklong stays with my grandparents, it was perhaps the first time in my life that I had been away from home and my parents overnight. We swam every day in the park's pool. More exciting, though, was our hiding our club leader's corset. As I look back, considering Miss Gert Lewis's willingness to leave her comfortable home for life in a primitive cabin with unruly girls, that was not a nice thing to do. But it was fun!

Unfortunately, my 4-H experience would be limited. My parents sold our farm in the spring of 1946, and we moved into Atlantic, into a house they had purchased at 803 Walnut Street. At that time, Iowa 4-H policy precluded 4-H membership for town girls.

High School in Atlantic

I had completed my eighth year at Washington No. 4 in the spring of 1945, and that fall I enrolled for my freshman year at Atlantic High School. The Atlantic school district boundary was the city limits; townships paid tuition to the Atlantic district for their students, and there was no school transportation. Our farm was eight miles from town, so during the school week I shared a bedroom with my sister Norma Jean and her classmate Norma Jean Christensen in Mrs. Claussen's small one-story home at 907 Chestnut. Dad or Mr. Christensen would drive us to Atlantic on Sunday night or early Monday morning and pick us up at Mrs. Claussen's after school on Friday. We took our breakfast and dinner at Mrs. Claussen's and ate lunch at the school. That arrangement ended, of course, when my family moved into Atlantic the following March. Then I could walk home for lunch.

The Hansen family during my high school years. Younger sister, Marilyn on my left, Norma Jean far left.

Our house on 803 Walnut was but a block from Peace Evangelical Church, which our family had attended for many years; two blocks from Lincoln Elementary School, which my younger sister, Marilyn, would attend; and four blocks from the grocery store and other downtown stores. Dad had started a new job even before the family moved into town, assembling farm equipment at the relatively new John Deere dealership, Cappel's, at the north end of Chestnut Street.

I had been baptized in the Peace Evangelical Church in Walnut and later confirmed in the Atlantic church. During my high school years, I helped teach classes for preschool children and also sang a few times in our small church choir.

Life in town was far different, with no farm chores but more things to do. In the summer I would walk the ten blocks to Sunnyside Park and swim with friends; that began my lifelong love of swimming. On Saturday nights Rosetta Gustafson and I would walk to the Peterson family roller-skating rink, also on the west edge of town. An organist gave us a beautiful rhythm as we circled counterclockwise, Mr. Peterson skating among us, his whistle ready to call out any behavior that was out of line. Dad would pick up Rosetta and me about ten o'clock.

Though no longer in 4-H, I still wanted to see my former club members' projects at the county fair, so I would walk with friends to the opposite side of town to the fairgrounds, the east end of Fifth Street (that site now a trailer park). It was while walking through the fairgrounds in August before my junior year that a young man called out, "Hi, Shirley." I did not know who he was but learned he was a nice farm boy who attended Wiota's school. Duane had met my father when the latter had been out at the Acker farm helping assemble a forage chopper Duane's dad had purchased. He would be my future husband.

High School

I describe my Atlantic High School years as rather simple. I walked the six blocks to school, three south and three east, and often met Marianne Gunderman, who would become a lifelong friend, a block from the school. We both walked home for lunch, so we made round-trips twice a day. Occasionally, perhaps to celebrate having done well on a test, Marianne and I might walk down to Crabtree's on Chestnut Street for a soft-serve cone.

Each year I signed up to take Spanish, but there were never enough sign-ups for a class. I also hoped for a class in art, but that, too, was not offered. I joined the Girls Athletic Association and earned enough points roller-skating, swimming, and walking to be awarded an Atlantic A for my sweater. However, there were no interschool sports, such as basketball or softball, for girls.

At the end of my freshman year, I was selected to attend the Girl Reserves Conference, a weeklong August leadership workshop at Central College in Pella. Janet Reeves, a to-be senior, was the other attendee from Atlantic. Dad drove us to Pella; he enjoyed driving that 1939 Chevrolet.

The next summer, when I was to become a junior, along with three others from our church, I attended a weeklong Christian youth camp on the Dana College campus in Blair, Nebraska. Both were great experiences that allowed me to meet and know other teenagers from across Iowa and Nebraska.

The normal training program no longer offered, I chose the secretarial/business curriculum as a junior and took typing and shorthand, both taught by Miss Black, plus bookkeeping. I enjoyed all the courses, and they proved valuable. Miss Gladys Kluever, who had taught my Latin and math classes, asked if I would like to type and reproduce tests for her. She knew I could be trusted not to disclose questions to other students. Then, another teacher, Miss Cochran, asked me to type tests for her. These were not only good experiences, I also got paid!

The reader might ask, "Did you not consider a precollege curriculum?"

Thought of college was not in my realm. Until I was a freshman in Atlantic, I do not recall college being mentioned by any schoolmate, neighbor, or family member. Except for our minister and Dr. Wilder, who no doubt were college educated, I do not recall at this writing anyone I then knew who had gone off to college. It would only be in later years that I would learn that two of my father's sisters, then in Omaha and California, had each, for a time, attended Iowa State Teachers College (now the University of Northern Iowa). My teachers at Washington No. 4 had likely completed the normal training program as high school seniors.

Though I had dreamed of being a teacher and was likely aware in my later high school years that college would be a prerequisite for teaching in a city school, family finances would not let me think of attending college. For me and for most of my female peers, our options were nursing and secretarial.

Dancing at the Community Hall

Along with several others, I was invited after my sophomore year to attend dances arranged by a rural youth group and held at a community hall two miles south of Atlantic on US 71. By coincidence, Duane, then having finished his junior year at Wiota, had also been invited. It was an informal group, with roots in a post–high school organization called Link and Linkettes.

Dancing was to records, the record player borrowed from the county Farm Bureau office. There was a rare waltz, but most of the music was fox-trot. Many dances started with mixers, usually men facing the east wall, women the west. When the music started, all backed up toward the middle, and each danced with the person they bumped into. Or, in the middle of a dance, the women were called to form a circle and move clockwise, and the men created an outside circle moving counterclockwise. When the music stopped, each danced with the person facing. Of course, there would perhaps be a bit of nudging to align with the one you had your eye on.

Membership was listed in a shorthand notebook, and two couples served as a committee to plan the next dance, which included reserving the hall, arranging an older couple to chaperone, planning refreshments, and sending penny postcard notices to all. Near the end of the dance, the committee would name two other couples to plan the next dance.

At an early-September dance, a week or so after Duane's "Hi, Shirley" at the county fair, the committee for the next dance was announced: Don Stamp and his then steady date, Marlene Laartz, and Duane and me! No doubt our selection had been prompted by some of our friends.

A week later, Duane drove his 1929 Model A Ford to my house, where Don picked us up in his 1948 Ford Coupe (one of the first civilian models available after WWII), and we drove to the Laartz farm south of Anita to plan the next dance. From then on Duane and I were steady dates, for dances, skating, and movies.

By November, Duane's dad had traded both Duane's Model A and his own Model A "farm car" for a new Jeep. Except for its yellow color and aluminum cab, the Jeep was only slightly modified from the WWII version. The only problem was its high step, which was difficult for me when I was wearing a long dress. Duane added a radio, and his dad thoughtfully added a bridging cushion between the Jeep's two fixed seats. The bright-yellow Jeep meant that there was no community anonymity to our dating schedule.

My dad had not taught me to drive. While teaching Norma Jean in his yet new Chevrolet, she had not slowed enough turning in our drive and had hit a gatepost rather squarely. Perhaps he was not willing to take a chance with me as a result of this incident.

One Sunday afternoon, Duane drove us down to his family's pasture, put the Jeep in low range, and said, "You drive!" It was wonderful. Other than a few grazing cows, there was nothing to hit. In low-range first gear, I could gradually get the feel of handling the steering, shifting gears, braking, backing up, and all that goes with driving. After a few afternoons in the Acker pasture, I felt totally comfortable, even in high range and on the road.

The Popcorn Company

The summer after my junior year, the president of a local popcorn company asked me to fill in, typing letters and answering the phone, while his secretary was on vacation. Apparently my typing and shorthand instructor, Miss Black, had suggested me. The company office was a little cement block structure several blocks northwest of Atlantic's downtown, across the Rock Island tracks from the Swift and Company egg and milk receiving plant, and ten blocks from our home. Dad, working at Cappel's, on the north end of Chestnut Street, drove me to and from work.

Perhaps Miss Black had also suggested me to the hospital superintendent, as he asked me to do the same a few days that summer. Both were great experiences.

Dental Assistant

In late winter of my senior year, a neighbor, Gayle Johnson, asked if I would be interested in replacing her as assistant to a local dentist, Dr. Ellender. She was moving to another job. I interviewed, was hired, and went in after school and on Saturdays for Gayle to show me what the work entailed. She even gave me her white uniforms, and Mother remodeled them to fit me.

I started full-time on the Saturday morning after Friday-night graduation, and Dr. Ellender had a full schedule for the day. Though I felt prepared and was proud in my white uniform, I probably wondered, *Will I get the patient's bib on right? When Dr. Ellender asks for a certain tool, will I be able to hand him the right one?*

One of the first procedures that first Saturday was for a little girl by the name of Kay. I know now it had to have been Marcella Kay Jensen, who would be, forty-five years later, our farm neighbor and friend.

Yes, it was a busy day—eight or ten patients for fillings, an extraction, and even a denture fitting, with several of the appointments taking more than an hour. For me the day went well. There were no crises, and I was eager to be back in the office Monday morning.

The work was varied and interesting. I helped Dr. Ellender with the x-rays and then did the developing. I also mixed the components for silver or gold fillings and removed the mercury from the mix. Plastic fillings had also become available, and I enjoyed matching the color of the filling material with the patient's tooth enamel. Perhaps this was my artistic interest coming through.

On several occasions I prepared the plaster of paris Dr. Ellender used as a mold for dentures. After the plaster impression hardened, I would clean and smooth the impression and take it across the street to an upstairs shop that made bridges and dentures. A few days later I would pick up the finished item, making sure it was clean and ready. I thoroughly enjoyed the work, even the task of sterilizing the instruments after use.

Just before lunch on Wednesday of my first week, Dr. Ellender gave me another task, one that I had not expected. There would be no patients that afternoon (most dentists, optometrists, and physicians then took Wednesday afternoons off, perhaps for golf but also to compensate for full days on Saturdays), so he asked that I try to collect some overdue accounts, by phone and by calling on the patient. Though not comfortable with the task, I made the calls and knocked on a few doors. I do not recall that I brought back any cash or checks, but the patients I visited were most gracious.

Late July brought another surprise, a feature I had not learned when I took the job. Dr. Ellender would leave late summer for a month's vacation, and though I would need to be in the office every day to handle calls, pick up the mail, and arrange future appointments, as well as collect past bills, he told me I would get only half pay while he was gone. I was stunned and felt I had been misled.

Walnut Grove

The weekend after finding out about the half pay, I learned from Duane's sister Lorraine that Walnut Grove Products Company, a local feed manufacturer where she worked and that was known for its good pay scale, needed a typist. I interviewed, learned the job would be more than typing, was offered the position, and quickly accepted. The next morning I told Dr. Ellender that I would be resigning at the end of the week.

I regretted leaving the dental office. I loved the work. It was interesting and let me make use of my artistic interests, and I could have enjoyed it as a career. However, I needed the steady income and felt fully justified in making the change. Further, my new salary would be higher than at the dental office, and health insurance was included.

The Sales Manager Needs a Steno

A few weeks into my new job, when I was barely comfortable with my work, the office manager, Mary Lang, came by my desk. Our experienced stenographer was absent that day, and the sales manager, Howard Herbert, needed some steno work done. "You took shorthand in high school," Mary said to me. "Can you take a letter for Herb?" Before I could explain that shorthand had not been my favorite subject and I had not used it since, Mary closed the issue by saying, "He's ready for you."

I would later learn that Herb was a kind and gentle soul. However, at this time, all I knew was that he was the apparent number two in the company and in his sixties; I was only seventeen and new to the business.

I grabbed a pencil and tablet and headed for his office, shaking a bit. I was hardly inside his office door when he started dictating. I jotted down the addressee's name, tried to recall and scribble the symbols that stood for pounds, product, cattle, illness, or whatever Herbert was talking about. When he quit talking, he gave me the letter or note related to his dictating, and I backed out of his office to the security of my desk. I put a sheet of Walnut Grove letterhead in my typewriter, but I had no idea the full meaning of what I had written down.

I asked Mary for help. She knew enough about the business and Herbert's terminology that, between the two of us, we were able to craft the body of Herbert's letter. I typed it, she took it to Herbert, and he signed it. I relaxed.

My job was to record salesmen's reported sales, calculate their sales commissions, and, after their commission checks had been signed by the company treasurer, mail the checks to them. I soon learned each salesman's location, who sold the most product, and which products sold in greater volume. When salesmen visited the home office, I could relate the name to the face and mannerisms and make some judgment about why some led others in sales. After meeting many, I felt a responsibility to them and sometimes worked Saturday mornings to get their checks in the mail.

I especially enjoyed my daily interaction with the other five or six gals in the office. We had fun and not just during coffee breaks. Though we sometimes brought our lunch, especially in winter, several of us would often would walk together the three or so blocks to a downtown café.

I arrived at Walnut Grove about the time the company expanded its product line from only livestock minerals to what was called complete-ration "supplements," containing vitamins and high-protein ingredients, such as soybean meal, in addition to minerals. There would be supplements for beef cattle, dairy cattle, swine, and poultry. A new name for these supplements was to be coined and a new bag designed. (Duane, then working at the new Walnut

Grove research farm would sit in on the brainstorming for that new name, and he describes the experience in *From Troublesome Creek*.)

Mary knew of my artistic interests, and once the new name—*4x4*—had been chosen, she asked if I would sketch several possible designs for presenting *4x4* on a feed bag. I take no credit for the final design that would eventually appear not only on Walnut Grove bags but also emblazoned on delivery trucks in the company's seven-state region. But it was fun to sketch some possibilities.

Duane had gone off to Iowa State in September of my senior year, so, except for his weekends and holiday vacations at home, my focus that year had to be school. For a few of his FarmHouse fraternity parties, homecoming, and VEISHEA, I was able to get to Ames, sometimes driving with Lorraine or other Atlantic girls. For two Saturday-night events, Dad made arrangements for me to fly from Atlantic to Ames in the mail plane. Duane usually arranged for me to stay with other out-of-town FarmHouse girlfriends in the home of mathematics professor Ralph Anderson and his wife, at the south end of Lynn Avenue, about four blocks from FarmHouse.

We could date more during the summers. Duane was home for farm work the first summer, and the second summer he lived at home and worked as an extension 4-H assistant in nearby Audubon County. The third summer, 1951, he was at Atlantic's new radio station, KJAN, for a few weeks, then helped build pens and facilities for Walnut Grove's new research farm southwest of Atlantic.

Marriage and Pammel Court

Duane, who had developed interest in graduate study in animal nutrition, would graduate at the end of winter quarter, March 1952, and continue on toward a master's degree. We therefore planned our wedding for March 23, the Sunday after his Friday-morning graduation. His to-be major professor, Damon Catron, had offered me a typing job in his office. With an $18-per-month two-bedroom unit in a Pammel Court Quonset, Duane's $125-per-month assistantship provided by Walnut Grove, and my $135-per-month salary, we were all set.

A heavy snow on Saturday, March 22, blocked many country roads, and even the highways were getting snow packed. Duane stayed in town Saturday night with his sister to ensure his presence for our ceremony at the First United Methodist Church in Atlantic. A few friends were not able to attend, but the wedding party was complete, and the wedding and the reception following in the church basement went off without a hitch.

The traditional first serving of cake to the bride at our wedding reception in the basement of the First United Methodist Church in Atlantic. As chocolate lovers, we had asked that one layer of the cake be chocolate.

At the close of the reception, Duane drove me down the hill and around the corner to my home on Walnut Street so I could change into my honeymoon outfit. He let me out at a path shoveled to the curb, then drove forward so others of the party could make use of the path. His thoughtfulness was a mistake. My brother-in-law Glenn Owen Jones and Duane's fraternity brother Regis Voss, in the next car, drove forward. Regis grabbed and pulled me into their car, and Glenn took off, up the street and around the corner. There was no way that Duane, by then out of his car with his keys in his pocket, could follow or catch up. They took me to a restaurant on the west edge of Atlantic, set me up on the counter—still in my wedding gown—and suggested I beg or bark like a dog and they might take me back to Walnut Street.

Duane was waiting for me at my parents' home when Glenn and Regis brought me back. In the meantime, he had driven to a local service station to have chains put on his 1949 Ford so we could safely drive out of town. We planned to drive to Des Moines's premier hotel, the Fort Des Moines, but US

6 was snow packed and slick, making driving treacherous. We eventually gave up and checked into a motel on the west edge of Adel. We would drive on to Des Moines the next morning.

We had but three days for a honeymoon before spring quarter classes and my new job would begin. Guy Lombardo's Royal Canadians were playing at nearby KRNT Theater, so we got tickets for Monday night. We enjoyed the concert, and visiting with band members in the hotel elevator was a bonus.

On Tuesday we purchased an unfinished chest to complete what was needed to fully furnish our tiny Pammel Court home. Duane had purchased a small stove and couch from the Quonset's previous occupants, his parents had loaned us a bed, and we had purchased a 6.2-cubic-foot refrigerator with money I had saved. A kitchen table set, living room chair, and pole lamp, all wedding presents, would pretty well fill the small two-bedroom unit. On Wednesday morning, with the unfinished chest of drawers in the back seat of the Ford, we headed to Ames and our first home, the Iowa State Pammel Court Quonset.

* * * * *

On earlier pages I mentioned the goals that Duane and I set early in our Kansas State presidential years, outlining the major things we wanted to do or experience in the balance of our lives. High on my list was to visit foreign countries I had not seen. I had then been only to Canada and several European countries. During those presidential years and our time in DC, I had the opportunity to see parts of Nigeria, Kenya, Botswana, South Africa, Australia, New Zealand, the Philippines, Taiwan, Japan, Mexico, China, Israel, Morocco, Norway, Sweden, Denmark, and the city-state of Hong Kong. These were wonderful experiences, but there was more to see.

CHAPTER 9

More of the World to See

Life on our Iowa farm did not preclude travel. Duane had long been a member of a national agricultural roundtable, a mixture of producers, related business people, and a few academics, and there were three-day events twice a year, in each case a one-day tour of the host area's production or processing and two days of discussion. Because of Duane's experiences and relationships, he was also called upon for some domestic and international consulting and advising. When circumstances permitted, I joined him, especially if it involved work in countries I had not visited.

Here are synopses of some of our travels since moving to our farm.

Belarus, November, 1993

Duane was asked by Volunteers in Overseas Cooperative Assistance (VOCA) to spend a month in Belarus, one of the former Soviet republics, lecturing to university students on what private farming was all about. He would be joined by Dale Seebach, a college classmate and former extension agent in neighboring Shelby County. Though it was a volunteer assignment, VOCA provided travel expenses for both lecturers and their spouses.

At this time, each of the former Soviet republics was trying to move away from central government (Moscow) control. The citizenry of each republic, especially college faculty and government leaders, were trying to understand private enterprise. There was little or no private infrastructure to provide farm inputs or market farm products, farmland ownership had not yet been legislatively authorized, a taxation system to finance government expenditures was not yet in place, and inflation was rampant. Duane's memoir *Back to Troublesome Creek* more fully describes our time in Belarus; I include here a few condensed excerpts.

Two VOCA staff met us at the Minsk airport and took the four of us and our luggage in two small cars to a hotel, perhaps five kilometers from the city center. Our room was cold! We found only a bit of heat drifting from a recessed radiator below the hotel room window. We stacked two chairs over the lukewarm radiator and against the window drapes to block cold oozing in from outside, crawled under heavy blankets, and slept. We breakfasted the next morning in our room on dried fruit and granola from our suitcase, then walked to an adjacent supermarket to purchase a loaf of dark bread and to seek, without success, bottled water "without gas" (noncarbonated).

After a late-morning briefing in the downtown VOCA office, our university host took us to the campus for lunch. Considered special guests, we were accommodated in a dining room just off the student-faculty cafeteria. Windows lined one side of the cafeteria, and it was even colder than our fifty-five-degree hotel room. The menu was cabbage borscht, beet-and-cabbage salad, hot dogs cooked in butter, french fries, and hot tea. It was excellent food and flavorful. Within our host's resources, we were being treated beautifully and felt complimented.

We were taken to one of the few private farms in the country so Duane and his colleague could have a base for preparing their lectures about what students might encounter as private farmers. The government had "allocated" twenty-three hectares (about fifty acres) from a collective farm three years earlier and another twenty-three hectares the year of our visit to a forty-year-old former truck driver who had "always wanted to farm."

A cement block barn held twenty-four Holstein-Friesian cows, several calves, a dozen sows with litters of six to nine pigs, two horses, about twenty sheep of mixed breeding, and about twenty-five hens of mixed color. The major crops were potatoes and barley.

The farmer did not hold title to the land, so it could not be sold, but it could be passed on to the next generation. With land at no cost, a government operating loan of 2,000 rubles per hectare at 2 percent interest for three years, and inflation at 1,000 percent, he had a great deal! He would eventually pay off his loan with cheaper rubles and, in the meantime, pay little interest.

Back in Minsk the next day, Carol Seebach and I stood in the bread line at a supermarket with Belarus women. Every hour, another batch of loaves would come out of the market's oven, be placed on the shelves, and be quickly snapped up by the shoppers. Elsewhere in the store, some shelves were bare. In the canned fruit section, all we could find were jars of applesauce.

Local hosts escorted us to a performance of *Swan Lake* and also to the Minsk Museum. At the latter's shop, I could not resist purchasing a large bright-red vase with gold design.

Our interpreter, a retired military man on the English faculty, invited us to a Sunday-afternoon visit and tea with him and his wife in their tiny apartment in a Minsk suburb. Though cozy and comfortable, the apartment had a total square footage that was less than that of our Quonset unit in Iowa State's Pammel Court. Rampant inflation had made his military retirement pay virtually worthless and his university pay hardly enough to buy food. Layers of carpet on the floor and a carpet hung on the wall likely represented much of their worldly possessions and also helped keep the apartment warm. Regardless, their hospitality was generous. He wanted to give us a gift and presented the Seebachs and us each with a book from his personal library. We could not refuse.

Costa Rica with Iowa State, March, 1994

Duane was serving as part of an Iowa State University team that would spend a week with University of Costa Rica agriculture faculty reviewing their work both in San Jose and at farms and research facilities in rural Costa Rica. Several other spouses and I were invited to go along. We visited pineapple and sugar plantations, a producer of ornamentals, the Carara Biological Reserve near the west coast, and the International Institute for Cooperation in Agriculture near San Jose. Duane and I had visited other such research institutes in the Philippines, Nigeria, and Kenya in earlier years. Here we listened to staff describe their work in a tropical environment with cereal crops, tropical fruits, animal diseases, and even human nutrition.

* * * * *

When Duane reached sixty-five and became eligible for Social Security (SS) payments, tax policy was such that our net farm income (earned income) voided any SS payments, yet he would pay SS tax on that income. Rent income, however, was deemed passive income, so that policy did not apply. With strong demand by other farmers for land to rent, it made economic sense to close down our farming operation and rent the land to others. We then had more time to travel.

We took a combination plane/cruise trip to Alaska in the late summer of 1996, our last farm-operating year. We enjoyed the trip and decided to plan at least two major travels each year, one domestic and one foreign.

Upper Amazon and Machu Picchu

In March 1997, Duane and I flew from Miami to Iquitos, Peru, to join twenty others and a National Wildlife Federation expedition leader for, first, a weeklong cruise on the Upper Amazon. With tight but comfortable accommodations on a riverboat, *La Turmalina*, we headed upriver. Two guides, both with degrees in tropical tourism, were among the fifteen-member crew. The Amazon is the world's second-longest river and one of the deepest. With its tropical, high-rainfall watershed, it carries more water than any other.

It was flood season, so the river itself was evident only by the river's current and bordering vegetation. During the day we could watch river traffic, mostly native Quechua Indian families transporting bananas, vegetables, and other fruit downriver to villages or Iquitos. Though the water was unpolluted, with no industrial or city waste, it appeared almost black, due to tannin from the live and decomposing trees. At night, away from the river current, the water surface was like a mirror. From *La Turmalina* or any smaller boat, we seemed to be floating in space among endless tree trunks. Except for the moon, there was total darkness—no city lights on the horizon and no jet plane lights crossing the sky. A few nights, we disembarked from *La Turmalina* to small boats. We floated among the water-surrounded trees, listened to the natural sounds of the tropical night, and, with flashlights, caught the activity of native animal and bird species.

Each day we would disembark to tour a native village or to board small boats to get a closer look at tropical flora and fauna. We fished for piranhas, each of us with a string and hook on the end of a stick and a small piece of meat as bait. As soon as the bait hit the water, it was attacked by a swarm of those small fish and was gone in seconds. We had piranha for dinner that evening, and it was flavorful.

On a tributary of the Amazon near Iquitos, in northern Peru, March, 1997.

Floating among the flood-engulfed trees, we had close-up views of three-toed sloths, long-nosed bats, parakeets, parrots, and green tree iguanas. Perhaps the most fascinating were the lives and antics of several species of monkeys, ranging from a half pound to twenty pounds. We saw many bird species, from hummingbirds and fork-tailed flycatchers to hoatzins and kingfishers to red-bellied macaws and toucans. We expected the many bird and animal species but were surprised to find dolphins, referred to as pink river dolphins.

After the Amazon was a two-day bus ride through Peru's upland farming valleys and then, on a Sunday, up the mountains to a native Quechua village at an altitude of twelve thousand feet. We had taken bags of bread and some fruit as gifts, and our hosts showed much appreciation. Though the area was a barren landscape, seemingly above the tree line, the homes were made of wood. We moved slowly and with some difficulty in that rare atmosphere, but the native children were engaged in a vigorous running game.

We spent the night at the foot of the mountains, an area rich with flower gardens, hummingbirds, and butterflies. Early morning we were ready, after a cup of tea, for a bus trip winding up another mountain to the "Lost City of the Incas," Machu Picchu. The terraces and watercourse structures, covering a massive area of mountainside and built with precision, were both humbling and awesome.

We then went down the mountain toward the historic city of Cusco. This time, instead of traveling by bus on a winding road, we traveled via zigzagging switchbacks in a two-car electric train. We first headed a thousand feet downslope going west. At a level stopping point, the engineer went to the opposite end of the train and piloted us a thousand feet downslope going east. After perhaps a half dozen of these switchback segments, we were at the edge of Cusco, the historic trade center of the Incas.

I enjoyed the Upper Amazon so much that when my daughter LuAnn expressed interest three years later, I joined her for a repeat experience.

Europe by Train, July and August, 1998

Diane and Terry had rented a home in Switzerland for several weeks, so Duane and I planned a two-week Eurail Pass that would include a day with them. LuAnn joined us for the first several days of our trip, during which we took a train from Paris to Venice, explored the canals of Venice, and then visited Rome and the vicinity. LuAnn flew home early in the morning from Rome, and Duane and I headed to the train station for a ride through the Alps to Geneva.

A half hour out of Rome, noticing a number of dark-complexioned riders, Duane asked one, "Where are you headed?" The answer was "Home to Tunisia!"

We had misread the marquee and had boarded on the wrong track. We pulled out our map; the next stop was Naples, close to Pompeii. We had never been to Pompeii; now was the time! At the Naples station we put our luggage in a locker, purchased a large bottle of water at a McDonalds, and boarded a local interurban train to Pompeii. That afternoon we walked Pompeii's streets and viewed the remaining frescoed walls of homes and stores buried by the ashes of Mount Vesuvius in AD 79.

Back in Rome that evening, we found the right track for an overnight train to Geneva.

After several days with the Nygaard family, including a day train trip to Nice, France, with our grandsons, Eric and Clay, we were back on the train toward days in Vienna and waltz music. Then, it was on to Budapest, its late-1800s subway, and a live performance of *Oklahoma*. For each city we had reserved hotels within walking distance of the train station.

We then backtracked to several spots in southern Germany. In all we had twenty-two legs of train travel in the two weeks.

To China with Iowa State, September, 1998

Iowa State invited Duane to be among five current and former faculty to present lectures to faculty and students at three universities in China. Having been to China in 1980, I was glad to accompany the group and see how the country had changed.

After an overnight in Tokyo and an early-morning flight to Shanghai and Hangzhou, we found accommodations in a residence hall at Hangzhou Agricultural University. Two days later we flew on through Guangzhou to Wuhan and its agricultural university. In that university's laboratories we watched swine geneticists working with genetic code (genetic engineering) and communicating via email with their counterparts in the US and Europe.

Beijing was our last stop, and when I saw the facade and the surrounding grounds of our scheduled hotel, I sensed that I had been there before! Yes, though the grounds were more neatly maintained and the hotel lobby and rooms had been updated, this was where my People to People group had headquartered for our several-day Beijing visit in 1980.

*In Tiananmen Square, Beijing, September, 1998. It was
the second visit for me, the third for Duane.*

I took away several major impressions of China in 1998 as compared to my previous visit. First, I recognized that China's interior cities, such as Wuhan or Hangzhou, which I had not considered to be major cities, had three

145

to seven million people, populations comparable to Chicago or Los Angeles. I also recall the generous volume and diversity of meats, vegetables, and fruit for sale in booths at a Saturday-morning farmers' market near Wuhan's university campus. There were impressive two- and three-story homes just outside Wuhan. Our guide told us these were homes of rich farmers. These developments seemed a sign that capitalism was at work within this communist country. The many construction cranes in Beijing and elsewhere signified that much construction was underway. The four-lane highway to the Great Wall was far different from the narrow road we had traveled eighteen years earlier.

Calgary and Banff, Canada, June, 1999

In 1999 Duane and I traveled to Banff for a meeting of the agriculture roundtable, including a visit to an elk production farm just north of Calgary. Enroute to Banff, we drove a circuitous route through Oregon and Washington, then north through glacier country of the Rocky Mountains to Jasper and Edmonton's massive shopping center.

Brazil, Argentina, and Chile, February, 2000

Soybean production had exploded in Brazil, encouraged in part by the US embargo on exports to China, which had caused that country to turn to Brazil for soybeans. The explosion told us Brazil and Argentina, each with vast acreages of good soil, would be continuing competitors in the global grain market. We wanted to see for ourselves what our competition was up to, so we signed up for a two-week agriculture tour of Brazil, Argentina, and Chile, with most of the group being California Farm Bureau members.

In Brazil we enjoyed beaches and sugarloaf in Rio de Janeiro, then headed south to a longtime soybean, corn, and coffee production area and a soybean research center.

We took a flight to Iguazú Falls, a collection of 275 different cataracts where Brazil, Argentina, and Paraguay meet.

In Argentina we had dinner with the minister of agriculture, whose private farming corporation produced corn, soybeans, wheat, and sunflowers on two hundred thousand hectares between Buenos Aires and the Andes. We took a

Sunday ranch visit south of Buenos Aires, and in the evening we attended an Asado, with roasted lamb and trimmings.

After a flight to Bariloche, at the Andes foothills, we had a daylong alternating bus and lake-boat trip through the Andes to fruit country of southern Chile.

In Chile we saw cranberry harvesting, the venture a part of the US company Ocean Spray. We had a picnic on a dairy farm and explored the seashore near Santiago.

Nova Scotia and Prince Edward Island, September, 2000

We rented a car at the Boston airport, and from South Portland, Maine, ferried across a bit of the Atlantic Ocean to Yarmouth, Nova Scotia. Among highlights of our three days there were quaint villages, comfortable bed-and-breakfasts, a backcountry road sign for Acker Lane, the barren cliffs where some fuselage remnants and a memorial remind one of the 1998 Swiss Air Flight 111 that crashed nearby, and Cobequid Bay on the island's north side. The bay's narrowing feature results in the largest tide known.

Then we traveled across a new bridge to Prince Edward Island, where we saw rocky shores, a lighthouse on the point at Glace Bay, a whale being landed at a small village on the north shore, potato farms, a potato museum, and the home and history of Anne of Green Gables.

The return drive through New Brunswick included an egg farm and a provincial farm credit office, with farmer financing comparable to the US farm credit system.

Galapagos, January, 2001

I am a nature lover and always eager to see indigenous wildlife and birds. After two visits to Africa's Serengeti and my two weeks on the Amazon, there remained for me what many consider the zenith of nature viewing: the Galápagos Islands. My sister Norma Jean and I were among forty-two people on a tour arranged by the Iowa State University Alumni Association.

Our ninety-minute flight from Guayaquil, Ecuador, took us to Baltra Island for transfer to the cruise ship *Polaris*. The *Polaris* took us to several of the islands and also was our sleeping and meals headquarters. We disembarked each day to nineteen-foot Zodiacs and were then deposited on the islands with our tour guides.

Charles Darwin's theory of evolution, that humans came from what we know as other species, such as chimpanzees or apes, is based in part on his time on the Galápagos in 1835. There he searched for fossils and studied the many species of plants and animals.

I will not bother the reader with our day-by-day schedule on the several islands. Rather, I will list some of the species we had the privilege to identify and watch up close in their native habitat. Among the birds were blue-footed boobies, red-breasted frigates, magnificent frigates, swallow-tailed gulls, American oystercatchers, lava herons, hawks, and Nazca boobies. Among the sea species were sea lions, giant tortoises, teal-blue and red iguanas, large green sea turtles, crabs, porpoises, Bryde's whales, penguins, fur seals, and, of course, many fish species.

The island surfaces were largely sand and large and small rocks, with little soil—not easy walking. Many of the land-based animals, such as iguanas, seemed to blend in with their habitat, so we needed to watch our step.

We spent a day or more at the Charles Darwin Research Station on Santa Cruz Island, and perhaps my most vivid memory of the trip is the station's giant tortoises.

Belize, March, 2002

To celebrate our fiftieth wedding anniversary, Duane and I reserved two units for two weeks at Caribbean Villas on Ambergris Caye, a small island off the coast of Belize. LuAnn and her husband, Scott, would be our guests the first week, and Diane, Terry, and the twins, Eric and Clay, would be our guests the second week.

The villas were owned by Will and Sue Lala, with whom I had worked in the Manhattan Civic Theatre. Will had also been my dentist and, as a worker of metals, had designed and made for me both a ring and a pendant. During his years as a Manhattan dentist, he and Sue had spent many weeks as volunteer professionals at a clinic on the caye and, in time, had purchased this beachfront property, six rental units and a home.

Ambergris is a twenty-minute flight from Belize City. Its only city, San Pedro, stretches perhaps a mile along the gulf coast, three blocks deep at its widest, and our villa was near the south end. Transportation on the island was limited to golf carts, bicycles, and walking, except for a rare pickup that delivered orders to merchants and a John Deere tractor and a red wagon that took Coca-Cola products from the dock. Because the main street to the middle of town was being paved, all traffic from our end of town had to cross the airport runway. If a plane was ready to land or depart, a worker at the runway edge would lift a rope, tied at the far end to a post, in order to halt traffic.

Will escorted LuAnn, Scott, Duane, and me to Belize City, and we took a station wagon tour into the heart of Belize, including Mayan ruins, a private wildlife preserve, and a rich farming area complete with attractive dairy farms, a John Deere dealership, and milk processing cooperative, the latter a source of large ice cream cones. Later in the week, LuAnn, Scott, Duane and I flew across the Guatemalan border for our second visit to the major Mayan ruin Tikal.

Duane and I among major Mayan structures at Tikal in northeastern Guatemala.

For our second week, because of schedule conflicts, only Eric could be with us. The highlight of that week was the three of us fishing along the gulf, with a guide. We stopped midday, and our guide built a fire and prepared lunch using Eric's catch, with bread and vegetables to complement the fish.

Eric and Duane later rode bicycles to the far north end of San Pedro, where, to cross a small creek, they could board a "ferry." The ferry was simply a floating deck, perhaps twelve feet square, tied by rope to a tree upstream. The attendant would position a rudder under the ferry so that the current against the rudder would move the ferry to the opposite shore.

We recommend Belize and Ambergris Caye to those who seek a nearby "foreign" experience.

Hamburg to Saint Petersburg and Helsinki via Poland, September, 2002

Our daughter Diane joined us to visit my relatives in Hamburg and then on to Warsaw via Berlin. At Berlin's Ostbanhof station we had but twenty minutes for a midday transfer to a Warsaw-bound train. Duane stepped to a kiosk to purchase sandwiches, and he returned just as a train arrived on our Warsaw track. European trains arrive on time and depart on time, so we did not want to dally. Passengers disembarked; we grabbed our suitcases and jumped on.

We were just inside the car door when it closed and locked, and the train started moving! No one else had gotten on! We went to the next car—no one there, nor in the next. No attendant! No cord to pull!

Perhaps twenty minutes later, the train stopped, and the car doors unlocked. We opened the door and looked out ... and down. We were in a train storage yard on an elevated track, perhaps six feet above the ground. We spotted some workers on the far side of the yard and yelled for help. They looked up in surprise, clearly wondering, *What would people be doing on a train taken out of service?* Realizing our predicament, they rushed over, helped us and our luggage down to the ground, and led us to an interurban station platform at the edge of the yard. From there, a local took us back to Ostbanhof, where we boarded a six o'clock train for Warsaw.

We encountered more problems near midnight in Warsaw as we headed by taxi to a hotel we had been assured was mid-city. However, using our reservation address, our driver headed to the suburbs! We reversed course (we would deal with the faulty reservation later), and the taxi dropped us at the Marriott, where Duane had stayed in March. The Marriott had only one room available; we took it, and Diane slept on the floor.

We visited Warsaw's WWII ghetto, enjoyed an evening concert in the

Old Town, walked the city's fabulous Lazienki Park, and toured the massive Palace of Culture and Science, built by the Soviets in the 1950s. Diane flew home for work commitments, and Duane and I boarded an overnight train to Vilnius, Lithuania.

Though there was a direct rail line to Vilnius through a corner of Belarus, Belarus (again under some degree of Moscow influence) had refused to allow passage without visa inspection, so our timetable showed a longer route inside Lithuania. Early in the morning in Vilnius, we exchanged currency, walked the streets and parks, enjoyed sidewalk meals, and boarded another night train bound for Saint Petersburg.

We had been alerted to expect two visa inspections at the Latvia-Russian border, by each country's officials. About midnight the train stopped. Latvian customs officers boarded, entered our roomette, inspected our visas, ensured we matched our passport photos, and departed. Perhaps thirty minutes or an hour later, just as we'd fallen back asleep, the process was repeated by Russian officials.

Through a friend, Diane had arranged for a young woman to meet us at the Saint Petersburg station and serve as a helpful guide to the city for our two days there, including a visit to the well-known art museum, the Hermitage.

From Saint Petersburg it was an early-morning train ride to Helsinki, where we experienced a greater air of freedom. We walked the streets, enjoyed an evening concert in the Church in the Rock, and rode an airboat south across the Gulf of Finland for a day walking Tallinn, Estonia. We also wanted to see rural Finland, so for each of two days, we took a train north or northwest from Helsinki as far as we could and still catch a train back to Helsinki. At each end point, we walked the town, shopped, and visited with merchants. We captured a bit of Finland.

Wales and Scotland, May and June, 2004

To celebrate our grandson Clay's high school graduation, we scheduled a train trip with him from London along England's coast to Edinburgh and Inverness, Scotland, then back south to Wales. In Wales we would visit Talycoed, the estate and farm where Duane's Jones great-grandparents had lived and worked before coming to the US in the 1860s. Clay's parents, Diane and Terry, had identified a weeklong book festival in Hay-on-Wye, not far from Talycoed. They would rent a car in London and meet our train at Hereford, Wales, and we would all drive to a bed-and-breakfast at Llwynbrain, a dairy farm near Hay-on-Wye. We would enjoy both the book festival and Talycoed.

Highlights of the train trip included fields of brilliant blue blossoms of maturing flax and intermittent views of the English Channel. In Edinburgh, we enjoyed the Palace of Holyroodhouse, the official residence in Scotland of Her Majesty, the Queen; a description of historic cemetery robberies for gold tooth fillings; and an evening comedy club. On the train south from Inverness to Wales, Clay walked the cars to have conversations with fellow travelers.

In tents on the Hay-on-Wye fairgrounds, as well as in a few nearby churches or halls, authors presented the backgrounds and foci of their books, from fiction to humor to history of the Crusades, as well as related author experiences. The book festival had a county fair atmosphere, with food, authors' booths, and even demonstrations, such as sheep corralling by the author (and his dog) of a book on training sheepdogs.

We were later welcomed at Talycoed farm by the current owner. We walked the barns in which Duane's grandparents had worked, and we had tea and cakes in the current owner's farmhouse kitchen. We had visited the Talycoed estate years earlier but had missed the adjacent Talycoed farm. Both visits are described in more detail in Duane's *From Troublesome Creek*.

Greece and the Balkans, September, 2006

Beginning in Athens and ending in Zagreb, this two-week tour included seven countries that share the Dalmatian coast of the deep blue Adriatic Sea. By country, here are some impressions and observations.

In Greece, the highlight was Athens and its symbols of early democracy, including the Acropolis (at the top of the city), built about 3,000 BC, and the Parthenon, built about 440 BC. Athens was also home to the early Olympics. We visited a sixty-nine-thousand-seat stadium built for the 1896 Olympics that was also the site of the 2004 Olympics. The vast city of Athens, with its narrow streets, gave us our first view of today's Smart cars.

Entering Macedonia, the passport checkpoint was a small shack on a narrow road, seemingly isolated. I recall mountainous terrain, narrow roads, and small villages. We enjoyed Lake Ohrid and attractive lakeside resorts.

At the time of our visit, Albania was the poorest country in Europe, emerging slowly from communism, political isolation, and lack of private property ownership and free enterprise. Hundreds of concrete bunkers dotted the countryside, especially near borders. We saw tiny farms and acreages, with every square foot in use for fruit, corn, or vegetables. Along the Adriatic coast were miles of new, nearly finished condos, packed tightly and short on parking space—likely a result of external money and no zoning. The people took pride in their capital city, Tirana, and its museum, a five-star Sheraton Hotel, and brightly colored buildings.

From Montenegro, my strongest memory is tile roofs on homes in coastal villages, tightly packed between the bright-blue Adriatic Sea and mountains. The country was newly independent, having gained its independence from Bosnia and Herzegovina on May 2, 2006.

For Bosnia, we passed through only a ten-kilometer coastal strip of the country.

In Croatia we visited Dubrovnik, an ancient and now popular coastal city with narrow streets, walkways, a pier, and shops in walled Old Dubrovnik plus vibrant new sections and a picturesque bay. We saw folk dancing in the nearby village of Cilipi, plus remaining evidence of civil war, including bullet-chipped walls and a windowless shell of a building. We visited open-air produce markets, Roman Emperor Diocletian's palace, and early ruins (a UNESCO World Heritage Site) in Split. Unique was a marine organ at the Zadar waterfront, where incoming waves pushed air through horizontal organ pipes of varied diameter, producing low tones.

We traveled along a new divided highway that had been built by Bechtel, a US company. The highway included three mountain tunnels, one three and a half miles long. Plitvice Lakes National Park, another UNESCO World Heritage Site, was a particular high point, with its series of sixteen terraced lakes in thickly wooded mountain terrain. There were a couple of waterfalls between lakes, including one 480 feet tall, but most of the lake terraces were simply dams built up over centuries by precipitated calcium carbonate and algae.

As we traveled to and from Plitvice Lakes, we saw considerable remaining evidence of ethnic civil war, including depopulation, abandoned farms, and vacant homes. In the war, the Croatian army had crushed rebellious Serbs; many of them had left and were now reticent to return.

We saw numerous autos from Scandinavian countries pulling small camping trailers, likely headed to some of the many coastal campgrounds.

Slovenia was filled with attractive farming country, with five to ten-acre fields of alfalfa, small grain (postharvest stubble evident), and corn, with silage harvesting underway. We saw modern farm equipment and fruit orchards. The roads were excellent. We could see snow on the distant peaks of the Julian (southern) Alps. The city of Bled, with an all-season resort and lake, was a home base for skiers. Ljubljana, Slovenia's capital city, boasted a university, an open-air market, and bridges over the Sava River.

We then bused back to Zagreb, capital city of Croatia, for a brief city tour and early-morning Air France flight to the US via Paris.

Iceland, August, 2007

At the end of a six-hour flight from Minneapolis, we arrived at the Reykjavik airport at about seven thirty in the morning and boarded a bus for a tour of the city. (Our hotel rooms would not be ready until noon.) We drove by aluminum smelting facilities and learned that the geothermal heat for which the country is known gives the country an economic opportunity. Aluminum ore is imported from Australia, and the finished aluminum is exported to Europe and elsewhere. We visited the waterfront, watched a fishing boat crew unloading their overnight catch, whiled away an hour with tea and pastries at a waterfront café, and then checked in at our hotel.

Iceland lies just below the Arctic Circle and is warmed by the Gulf Stream. At 440,000 square miles, it is about the size of Kentucky, and with about 350,000 people, it is the least densely populated of European countries. About two-thirds of the population live in or near Reykjavik. The early settlers were from Norway, but the country also has historic and continuing links to Denmark. Though English is spoken by all, Icelandic, most similar to Danish, is the official language. People dress like those of the US and Canada and are friendly. The sidewalks, streets, and parks are neat and clean.

There are no chimneys in Reykjavik or other Iceland communities (with one small community exception). Homes, churches, businesses, and schools are all heated by hot water, directly or indirectly, from deep underground. In the case of Reykjavik, a conversion facility a few kilometers from the city uses the superhot, high-sulfur-content water from underground to heat fresh water from a nearby lake. The latter water is then moved for distribution in Reykjavik via a large-diameter pipe.

Our tour route, by bus, circumvented the island country. Much of the way, one row of farms lay between the two-lane highway and the ocean, and another row of farms lay between the highway and the mountains. A number of valleys did extend inward, hosting water streams from the mountains as well as farms and communities. The short growing season limits major crops to cereals and forages; long rows of white-plastic-covered round bales of hay (or haylage, wet hay that will ferment a bit in storage) let us know that cattle and sheep were the major livestock. Icelanders also eat and serve a lot of fish and lamb, and we found the latter very tasty.

The climate allows summer vegetable production, and the geothermal heat encourages greenhouse production year-round. Consequently, Icelanders raise and consume a lot of lettuce and other green vegetables. The low-cost heat has also prompted year-round flower production for the European market, and we visited such a business.

We visited two riding academies, one with a covered arena where young British girls were learning how to ride and handle the small stocky horses that are common in Iceland and one in open country, with a line of mounted girls exploring the countryside.

Outside of Reykjavik our accommodations ranged from a farm-located motel and restaurant to dormitories on a college campus. As in Reykjavik, all were excellent.

France, September, 2007

Though we had seen Paris and other parts of France, we had never visited Normandy. The day we returned from Iceland, we learned of a weeklong tour to France that included Normandy and parts of western France that we had not seen, and we signed up. The tour also included Mont-Saint-Michel, an island, with a one-time monastery, that was separated from the mainland only at high tide. It was the one tourist site Duane's father had visited during his deployment to France in WWI.

Among my lasting impressions of this France trip were the rugged terrain and the concrete fortifications that Allied troops had faced. I also recall the rows of crosses in both US and Canadian cemeteries, the quietness of the US cemetery, as well as Mont-Saint-Michel.

Vietnam and Cambodia, October, 2008

Duane and I were part of a joint Iowa State University and University of Iowa alumni group that traveled for two weeks in Vietnam and Cambodia. We departed Los Angeles and traveled, via Hong Kong, to, first, Hanoi, Vietnam. The first day, each of us passengers sat astride a whining motorbike, winding through throngs of residents before open-stall shops packed with merchandise. With webs of electrical, phone, and internet wires overhead, we had a rapid orientation to the reality of Vietnam. This and later experiences made clear to me that the Vietnamese are ambitious, enthusiastic, and entrepreneurial. Though they live and operate with Communist Party government leadership, they love the United States. To all our contacts in the country, the Vietnam War is history. And they have no love for China.

Our tour leader in the country was the son of a banker. He spoke English well and was not reticent to describe the family pain and consequences of the war, but, again, that was history to him. His focus, for himself, his family, and his country, was on moving forward.

We traveled the length of the country by bus and train, beginning with a Sunday luncheon cruise among the stone outcroppings in the Gulf of Tonkin. We visited a home, a family-operated café, an elementary school, and a community internet center in a small village. We progressed south through the long, narrow country via Hue and Da Nang (names familiar from the war years) and via Ho Chi Minh City (formerly Saigon) to the Mekong Delta. Along the way, while shopping for shoes in a small city, I could not find my size. The merchant hopped on his motorbike, headed to another shop, and was back in less than ten minutes with the correct size in the model I wanted. Entrepreneurship and customer service!

Perhaps most impressive was the delta, with its labyrinth of Mekong River channels by which people and commerce move. On a Saturday at Can Tho, we floated among dozens of farmers' boats loaded with vegetables and melons, local merchants shuttling from boat to boat negotiating purchases for their shops. In the more rural area of the delta, we off-loaded to waterside businesses, a fruit and ornamental "plantation," and a rice factory. At the rice factory, we watched a mix of rice grains and superheated sand, the rice being "popped" by the heat of the sand. The sand was then sifted out, and the popped rice was made into "rice krispie" bars, hand cut, and wrapped.

Later, outside of Ho Chi Minh City, we crawled into and through the Cu Chi tunnels, which Vietcong had dug and used during the war.

Then it was on to Siem Reap, Cambodia, and a floating village on nearby Lake Tonle Sap. On a boat, we passed dozens of floating homes (two were actually floating farmsteads, with a couple of pigs on feed), a school, and a basketball court and disembarked for snacks at a floating community market. Next we took a short ride north for a day at Angkor Wat, the "grandest of temples." Next it was on to Phnom Penh, the royal palace, and a brief visit to remnants of the brutal Khmer Rouge regime.

This, too, ranks as one of our most enjoyed travels. Though a far more contrasting culture than that of Iceland, the food, facilities, leadership, and accommodations were excellent, and we learned much.

East Berlin and Saschenhausen, March, 2011

I met daughter Diane and son-in-law Terry Nygaard for a week in what had been, in 1970, drab and depressing East Berlin. Germany's reunification after the post WWII Soviet controlled socialist "occupation" had yielded brightness and vibrancy. Streets were filled with autos and lined with new buildings; attractive shops were filled with merchandise and enthusiastic shoppers. Appliance features in their rented condo were a generation ahead of what Diane and I were using in the U.S.

Scabs of the Nazi era remained only in such as Saschenhausen Concentration Camp, which Terry and I visited and in which more than 100,000 Jews, communists, intellectuals, and gypsies had been killed between 1936 and 1945. Walking the streets from the rail head to the camp, the streets that most of those 100,000 or more had walked, and seeing the remaining barracks, gas chambers, and smokestacks were the most sobering of my experiences.

* * * * *

In recent years, we have not been as willing as in earlier years to take long flights with multiple connections. Though there are many parts of the globe we have not seen, our recent foreign destinations have been closer to the US. Moreover, we enjoy riverboats and trains, both of which let us view the landscape along the route.

Canals of Holland and Belgium, April, 2012

We went to Holland and Belgium with friends Bob and Judy Camblin in an Iowa State group. My most lasting impressions of the trip are fields of brilliantly colored tulips, the International Flower Festival, and the seawall that protects the Netherlands' lowlands.

The Great Lakes, July, 2012

We traveled from Chicago to Toronto via Lakes Michigan, Huron, Erie, and Ontario. The highlights of the trip include the sand dunes along Lake Michigan's eastern shore, Mackinac Island, Cleveland's iconic public buildings and its Rock and Roll Hall of Fame, Niagara Falls, and the fruit country of Quebec.

Panama and Costa Rica, February, 2014

Panama was a rich learning experience, including the fascinating canal history, the physical necessity for the original canal's series of locks at each end, and the lake that provides water source for the locks. Most impressive were the canal's high traffic volume, the size of the vessels going through the canal, and the massive lock gates being installed for the additional lanes then under construction.

For Costa Rica, my most vivid memories are of rugged grazing country, a tropical preserve, and small farms.

Train across Canada, October, 2015

We were part of an Elderhostel tour from Montreal to Vancouver via Toronto and Jasper. I was taken by the vastness of Canada's timberland and Great Plains, glaciers near Jasper, and Vancouver's residential/commercial communities encouraged by city planners.

* * * * *

At this writing we have not ruled out future foreign travel. However, we now more enjoy short, direct flights and, after those flights, unpacking in a comfortable room that will be our headquarters for a week. Riverboats fit the bill, with three meals a day, a view of the shoreline or country as we travel, day tours of cities and sites of interest, and evening entertainment. We have visited each of the following areas with American Cruise Lines, generally on ships of 125 to 160 guests.

Upper Mississippi, October, 2016
Puget Sound, June, 2017
Outer Banks, Jacksonville to Charleston, March, 2018
Columbia River, June, 2018
Hudson River, October, 2018
Lower Mississippi, March, 2019

We know not what experiences and travel lie ahead. Whatever they be, we will look forward to each and will find pleasure in every day.

CHAPTER 10

Concluding Thoughts

After gathering materials and memories, writing and re-writing, and then reviewing the several chapters, I have and share with the reader several thoughts that seem paramount.

I have even greater appreciation and respect for my parents, my sisters, the neighbors and classmates of my youth, and my early teachers. They gave me a solid base, a sense of right and wrong, loyalty to family and country, a work ethic, conservative values and habits, and the self-confidence to handle what comes.

Being less exposed during my early years to the "wider world," geography, other cultures, and the many professions and careers, I now realize there were two experiences that "opened the door" just a bit. The first was our two years living in Walnut, including a new friend and starting school in town. The second was the big city of Omaha, for family dinners and where, for church confirmation at age 11, I got my first store-bought outfit, a fuchsia wool suit (skirt and jacket). Though these experiences may seem mundane to others, I had learned there was, in fact, a wider world, more than our farm, family, and Washington No. 4.

This is a very wide world. My life has allowed me to realize how massive the geography, how diverse the world's cultures, and how dramatic its history. Further I understand the degree to which experiencing but a sample of this width broadened and enriched my perspective.

After watching a Botswana family hoeing weeds among sorghum plants and seeing the small metal canisters that would hold the harvest and supply their table between crops, while the man of the family was tending their few cattle on tribal grazing land, I better understood the tribal traditions and food limitations of much of central Africa.

Looking across loose rolls of barbed wire at gun-carrying soldiers in sentry towers atop "The Wall" on a Berlin Sunday morning in 1967, and later visiting the Normandy beaches and nearby U.S. and Canadian military cemeteries — and then Saschenhausen — fixed in me a fuller understanding of Nazi cruelty, WWII, as well as tragic post war consequences.

The drab dress and sad faces of people on the streets of Moscow, Russia, in the 1980s, and standing in line for bread "on the hour" in a Minsk, Belarus, supermarket told me more about the consequences of socialism than any piece I might have read in Time magazine or the daily newspaper.

Watching residents dig trenches for their own sewer system, the pipe provided by monetized food aid, showed me both the plight of some Central American families and the human value of U.S. food aid to such countries.

Having seen China sequentially, in 1980 and 1998, and later seeing the entrepreneurship and economic growth in neighboring Viet Nam, also a communist country, I comprehend how China could be on the way to out-distancing the U.S. as an economic power.

U.S. citizenship is precious. Our founding fathers, in the Declaration of Independence, the Constitution, and the Bill of Rights, put together an extraordinary guide for more than two centuries of un-interrupted human freedom, not the case on much of the globe. We have the freedom to learn, the freedom to be productive and to earn satisfactions in an occupation of our choice, freedom to associate and travel, and freedom to worship.

These documents also define a federation of states, with discrete powers to states vs. the federal government, a pattern followed at the state level and with sufficient local control at the county, city, or political district that every citizen can feel, "I count." I can vote; I can have an impact.

Observing unrest and disruptions in other countries (as well as in the U.S.) has reinforced for me that citizenship as not just a birth or naturalization certificate. It is knowing and respecting our founding documents, respecting the sanctity of the voting privilege, and, especially for those from other countries and cultures, it is assimilation into the society and mastering the common language, in our case, English.

Each of us is responsible for ourselves, regardless of economic status or family background. We may be guided and aided by parents, teachers, and others, but our health, satisfactions, and pride are largely determined by the extent to which we assume responsibility for ourselves, the decisions that each of us make.

Yes, government plays a role. Laws and regulations may encourage or constrain. And, there may be ethnic, religious, or other biases, or seemingly systematic barriers or constraints. However, in every circumstance, there are those who don't let those constraints unduly limit.

Every institution's strength depends on citizens who step up. Whether it be the local school, the church, the technical college, the civic organization, the charity, or the university, its ability to serve well its function depends largely on who and how many step forward to offer their time, their credibility, and their resources, whether as elected or appointed leaders or as private citizens.

It has been said, "The world is run by those who come to the meetings." That is too simplistic, but there is truth. Our life in several universities and several communities has reinforced that the basic ingredient is individual people who are willing to give of themselves to the good of the effort.

Every person needs love and attention. Whether it was the students' wives who found companionship in their organized club, the couple in Brookings for whom our Care Group arranged a golden wedding party, the university's renowned professor or the physical plant plumber, or the neighbor boy who just had to tell someone he had been elected class president, I have seen daily in my life the impact of a greeting, a positive word, a moment of recognition, or simply the evidence of belonging.

It can be said another way, "There are a lot of lonesome people in the world." This is especially true among the elderly, but also among both the wealthy and the poor, both the upper crust and the masses, both the physically strong and the infirm, and in both a populous environment such as DC and the house at the end of the country lane. So many of my life experiences have told me, "If you see a lonesome person, become their friend, if only for a moment."

* * * * *

My life has been richly blessed. I thank the reader for letting me share some of my experiences that helped make it so.

Printed in the United States
By Bookmasters